THE BIG BOOK OF

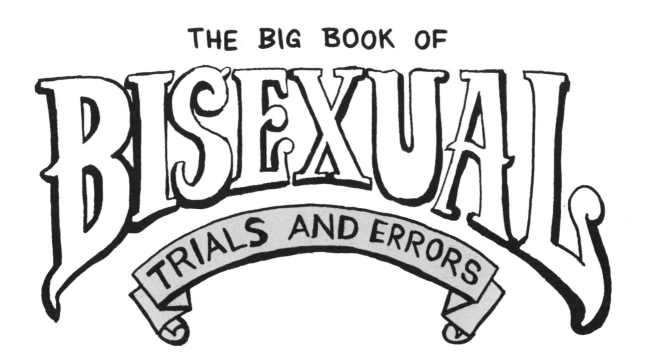

BISEXUAL

TRIALS AND ERRORS

BY ELIZABETH BEIER

Beier, Elizabeth
The Big Book of Bisexual Trials and Errors
ISBN-13: 978-1-943890-41-5

First printing, October 2017, by Northwest Press. Printed in Canada.

Table Of CONT...

NTS

FOREWORD
BY AVERY TRUFELMAN
OF ❯ 99% INVISIBLE

Avery Trufelman is a producer on the podcast *99% Invisible*, which focuses on the unnoticed architecture and design that shapes our world. Check it out at **99percentinvisible.org**

Elizabeth and I first met on OkCupid. It was back when we had both just graduated from college, both recently moved to California after breakups with serious boyfriends. I've never told her this, but it was the first time I publicly expressed that I was attracted to women. When I look back on it, I suppose that was how I came out: by clicking a preset option on a dating site.

Like many of our generation, Elizabeth and I were fortunate. We did not fear physical harm or ostracization from our liberal families, and we were encouraged to proudly proclaim our sexual orientation. The thing was, we were still trying to orient ourselves. We harbored different insecurities about being both accepted and desired by our LGBTQ community. We were figuring out how to date, how to present ourselves, and how to find comfort.

Our highest barriers, we realized, were our own self-doubts. The process of dispelling them has been confusing, messy, and riddled with heartbreak. After all, what is queerness but an embrace of the uncertain?

Bisexual Trials and Errors perfectly encapsulates this lifelong lesson. Elizabeth gives voice to those of us attempting to shake gendered stereotypes and aesthetics as we figure out who we are and who we want to give love to.

Yes, this is the story of one person's sexual identity, but it also the voyage of an artist. As Elizabeth grows from young girl to confident queer, the literal walls of her work come crumbling down; the lines and marks get bolder and more dynamic and the traditional comic book grids and portrait-based storytelling give way to the abstract, the strange, and the divine.

This collection is a rich interplay between the self, sexuality, and artistic practice. As much as we would like to state solidly and finally who we are, who we are attracted to, and what we make, these are three elements which will never be solid pillars. They are shifting sands, and that is their beauty.

So thanks, OkCupid. Bless your stupid heart.

—Avery Trufelman
  Oakland, CA, 2017

INTRODUCTION:

DRAW ME like one OF YOUR MEAN GIRLS

WHEN I WAS IN THIRD GRADE, I WAS CHUBBY...

...I WALKED WITH DUCK FEET...

...AND I HAD A SPEECH IMPEDIMENT THAT MADE ME SOUND LIKE A *DRUNK SEAL*.

DURING RECESS I LIKED TO WALK AROUND THE PERIMETER OF THE SCHOOL PLAYGROUND.

SOMETIMES OTHER KIDS WOULD ASK ME QUESTIONS LIKE...

WHAT GRADE ARE YOU IN?

...BECAUSE THEY KNEW I COULDN'T SAY WORDS WITH "R" SOUNDS.

HAHA

TEACHERS AND ADULTS GENERALLY *LIKED* ME.

THAT'S A GREAT DRAWING!

ONE RECESS AID, MRS. LEVI, WOULD SNEAK ME CANDY BARS...

YOU'RE WELCOME!

* "I'm allergic to chocolate."

... AND ENCOURAGE ME TO MAKE FRIENDS.

WHY DON'T YOU TRY PLAYING WITH THE OTHER GIRLS?

BUT I DIDN'T SEE WHY *I* SHOULD HAVE TO MAKE AN EFFORT TO BEFRIEND GIRLS WHO WERE MEAN TO ME...

WHAT'S YOUR LAST NAME?

WHAT DO YOU CALL *BIG RIDES* AT *THEME PARKS*?

WHAT'S A FLOWER WITH THORNS?

HA HA HA HA HA HA

... AND I DIDN'T MIND KEEPING MY OWN COMPANY.

ALL OF THIS CHANGED WHEN MY PARENTS DECIDED TO LET ME WATCH *TITANIC* ON VHS.

BUT ONLY BECAUSE YOUR DAD WORKED ON IT.

I SAW THAT JACK WANTED TO BE CLOSE TO ROSE, BUT AT FIRST SHE WAS LIKE...

oh no, I'm MUCH too fancy for you.

BUT THEN HE SHOWED HER HIS DRAWINGS...

...AND THEN HE DREW HER...

...AND THEN SHE LIKED HIM A *LOT!*

WHEN I RE-WATCHED THE MOVIE ON NETFLIX, I REALIZED...

WAIT, FUCK...

I'VE TRIED TO BE JACK FOR SIXTEEN YEARS!

I ALWAYS DREW PEOPLE I WANTED TO IMPRESS, ESPECIALLY IF I WAS ATTRACTED TO THEM. BUT JACK'S APPROACH DIDN'T WORK FOR ME ROMANTICALLY...

THANK YOU!

IT TOOK ANOTHER TWO YEARS TO FIGURE OUT WHY.

7

YEAH, I JUST GOT MARRIED. I SPENT MY WHOOOLE COLLEGE CAREER AND TWENTIES DATING WOMEN, BUT I MET THIS AMAZING, PROGRESSIVE, SMART, SEXY GUY AND...

YOU FELL IN LOVE?

I FELL IN LOVE. YEAH! SO I HAVEN'T BEEN TO A LESBIAN BAR IN AGES.

I WAS AFRAID PEOPLE WOULD BE... JUDGY.

BUT I MISSED BEING IN A QUEER SPACE.

I HEAR YA. I JUST BROKE UP WITH MY BOYFRIEND OF SIX YEARS AND MOST PEOPLE ASSUMED WE WERE STRAIGHT, EVEN THOUGH WE'RE ACTUALLY BOTH BI.

SIX YEARS! THAT'S A WHILE...

IF YOU HAD ASKED US BEFOREHAND WHO WE'D DATE IN COLLEGE, I WOULD HAVE SAID...

2007

I WANT A GIRLFRIEND WHO'S *BUTCH* AND *TOUGH*, LIKE P!NK THE SINGER...

OR JENNY SHIMIZU...

MEN

OR SHANE FROM THE L WORD.

AN ARROGANT AND *STERN* ATTITUDE IS ~~ACCEPTABLE~~ HOT.

SHE MUST *HATE* GEORGE W. BUSH AS MUCH AS I DO...

WAR IS TERROR

Give Peace Chance

...AND SHE MUST BE *CREATIVE*, A MUSICIAN OR WRITER MAYBE.

...ON THE OTHER HAND, I WANT TO BE AN ARTIST SO MAYBE SHE SHOULD BE PRE-MED WITH A CREATIVE HOBBY.

IDEALLY SHE WOULD HAVE SOME FIRST-HAND EXPERIENCE TO SUPPLEMENT WHAT I'VE STUDIED ONLINE AND AT THE LIBRARY.

THE WHOLE LESBIAN SEX BOOK

JAMES WOULD HAVE SAID...

UM. I DON'T REALLY *DATE*.

OUR NEW FRIENDS POKED FUN AT US...

YOU ARE *THE MOST* OBNOXIOUSLY ADORABLE COUPLE.

YEAH... WHEN'S THE WEDDING?

NO NO! I'M LIKE, 100% A LESBIAN. I'M <u>SUPER</u> GAY.

I LIKE... THAT GIRL, OVER THERE...

MHM.

AND JAMES IS LIKE... *VERY* CHRISTIAN, RIGHT? YOU SAID YOU DON'T BELIEVE IN DATING?

UH, YEAH.

I'M GONNA GO GET SOME TOTS. YOU WANT SOME?

YES PLEASE.

WE'RE *JUST FRIENDS!!!*

RIGHT...

O-KAY.

13

REGULARLY CRASHING OUT BY THE PIANO MADE US SORE...

... SO WE STARTED GIVING EACH OTHER MASSAGES...

... WITH DIFFERENT RHYTHMS, LIKE WITH THE MUSIC. SOMETIMES FAST AND CHOPPY LIKE RAIN...

... SOMETIMES SLOW AND DEEP, LIKE MOLDING CLAY...

... SOMETIMES THE BAREST WHISPER OF TRAILING FINGERS...

... SOMETIMES THE GOOD, HOT BURN OF RAKING NAILS.

WE DIDN'T EXPECT TO FIND OURSELVES IN THIS POSITION...

...BUT WE DEVOURED EACH OTHER.

JAMES STUCK WITH ME IN SENIOR YEAR WHEN I GOT SICK AND HAD TO TAKE TWO SEMESTERS OFF, SKYPING AND TEXTING EVERY DAY.

I JUST FEEL SO *BEHIND!* I HAVEN'T EVEN DRAWN ANYTHING IN MONTHS.

I KNOW, HON. BUT YOU'LL HEAL AND CATCH UP. I LOVE YOU.

I LOVE YOU TOO...

HE MOVED TO A SMALL TOWN IN MARYLAND FOR HIS FIRST JOB, AND I MOVED IN WITH HIM AFTER I GRADUATED...

...BUT I COULDN'T MAKE IT WORK THERE SO AFTER A YEAR I MOVED BACK WITH MY AWESOME FAMILY IN CALIFORNIA.

JAMES SAID HE WOULD MOVE TO SAN FRANCISCO ONCE I LANDED A DESIGN JOB, AND I WAS SURE WE'D GET MARRIED AND GROW OLD AND HAVE SIX GRANDCHILDREN...

...BUT THAT'S NOT HOW IT WORKED OUT. ONE MONTH INTO NEW JOB:

I JUST ... I LIKE MY JOB AND LIFE *HERE.*

AND I'M NOT SURE I WANT KIDS. I... DON'T ACTUALLY.

OKAY, SO... IT SOUNDS LIKE MAYBE WE SHOULD BREAK UP?

...YEAH.

.....

SO WE ENDED IT TWO WEEKS AGO, WHICH IS SAD, BUT... NOW I CAN FINALLY DATE WOMEN!

TWO WEEKS?!

YEAH... IT'S SOON, BUT I'VE GOTTA TRY! I FEEL LIKE WHAT JAMES AND I HAD WAS REAL. BUT THERE'S ALSO A VERY REAL PART OF ME THAT I'VE NEVER EXPLORED AND... THIS MIGHT SOUND WEIRD BUT...

... I FEEL LIKE IF I DON'T HAVE LESBIAN SEX, AND SOON, I'M GONNA EXPLODE.

HA HA! WELL, WELCOME TO THE LEXINGTON CLUB. I'M ACTUALLY REALLY EXCITED FOR YOU. I THINK WHEN YOU DO FIND A WOMAN WHO YOU... CONNECT WITH, THAT PART OF YOU WILL BECOME FULLY REALIZED AND IT'LL BE SO VALIDATING AND EXCITING.

HONESTLY... I BET IT'LL BE BETTER THAN YOU CAN IMAGINE BEFORE IT HAPPENS.

CHEERS TO THAT.

CLINK

17

RIKKI

JAN 20, '14

IT HAD BEEN SIX WEEKS SINCE THE BREAK UP...

oh...this.

FRAGILE

WHEN I GOT A MASSIVE CROSS-COUNTRY DELIVERY FROM JAMES.

hi E
this is most
of it. I hope
the lamps
are okay.
Love,
James

I KNEW GENERALLY WHAT WAS IN THE BOXES BUT I WASN'T READY TO OPEN THEM YET.

MY ROBE

MY OLD CLOTHES

OUR... THINGS

GREAT GRANDFATHER'S LAMPS →

BLACK HOLE

THE BOOKS FROM OUR SHELF

SO I GOT ONLINE, MADE A DATING PROFILE, AND PERUSED.

THE NUMBER OF HUMANS LOOKING TO CONNECT WAS STAGGERING.

I QUICKLY MADE A DATE WITH A WOMAN NAMED RIKKI. IT MADE ME LAUGH THAT SHE SAID SHE WAS REALLY GOOD AT "EVERYTHING."

cockybastard 1
30 · oakland · 75 % m

I'm really good at everything.

The first things peopl
Im very athletic.

21

SO THE NEXT DAY I PUT ON MY SEXIEST OUTFIT THAT WASN'T DIRTY...

...OOH YEAH, PLAIN BLACK SHIRT AND BLUE JEANS...

... WITH *HEELS*. WHICH I NEVER WORE WITH JAMES, BECAUSE I WAS TALLER THAN HIM.

ON THE BART TRAIN I TRIED TO PSYCH MYSELF UP FOR THIS ENCOUNTER.

OK SO IT DIDN'T WORK OUT WITH JAMES, BUT...

NOW YOU CAN FINALLY DATE THE WOMEN!

BEING SINGLE WILL BE FUN!

YOU'VE NEVER DATED AS AN ADULT... REALLY...

SO YEAH, IT ISN'T SO SAD...

AND YOU LOOK NICE THESE DAYS, SO, CONFIDENCE...

I MEAN, WHO'S HIPPER THAN A SINGLE, CUTE BISEXUAL?? NOBODY !!!

AND YOU HAVE ACCESS TO THE WHOLE BAY AREA!

AND THE INTERNET!

SO...BE HAPPY!

WE MET IN FRONT OF JUPITER, A BERKELEY SPOT. SHE HAD JUST SHOWERED AT THE GYM SO SHE SMELLED NICE.

HI—ELIZABETH? IT'S RIKKI. SORRY I'M LATE.

IT'S OK.

THEN WE WENT TO THE OUTDOOR SEATING AREA, WHICH IS LOVELY, TO LOOK AT THE MENU.

HM, I WONDER WHAT I CAN EAT HERE?

WE COULD SPLIT A PIZZA...

NO, I CAN'T EAT PIZZA.

ARE YOU SURE? THEY CAN MAKE THEM GLUTEN FREE OR VEGAN.

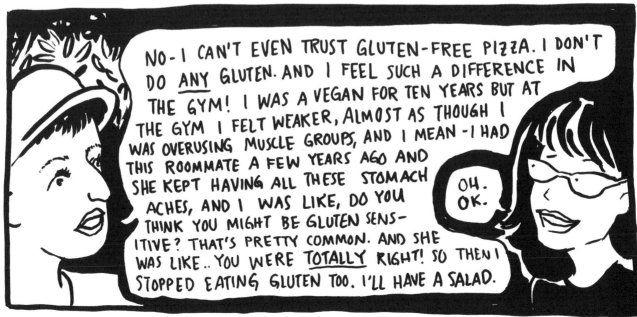

NO—I CAN'T EVEN TRUST GLUTEN-FREE PIZZA. I DON'T DO ANY GLUTEN. AND I FEEL SUCH A DIFFERENCE IN THE GYM! I WAS A VEGAN FOR TEN YEARS BUT AT THE GYM I FELT WEAKER, ALMOST AS THOUGH I WAS OVERUSING MUSCLE GROUPS, AND I MEAN—I HAD THIS ROOMMATE A FEW YEARS AGO AND SHE KEPT HAVING ALL THESE STOMACH ACHES, AND I WAS LIKE, DO YOU THINK YOU MIGHT BE GLUTEN SENSITIVE? THAT'S PRETTY COMMON. AND SHE WAS LIKE.. YOU WERE TOTALLY RIGHT! SO THEN I STOPPED EATING GLUTEN TOO. I'LL HAVE A SALAD.

OH. OK.

23

24

25

VIOLET

FEB 1, 2014

I MIGHT HAVE WRITTEN OFF OK CUPID AFTER RIKKI BUT THEN I GOT THE FOLLOWING MESSAGE:

YOU KNOW, I ALWAYS *WANT* TO DRAW PORTRAITS OF OTHER PEOPLE, BUT THEY ARE JUST SO RELUCTANT TO SIT STILL! I HAVE SOME BEAUTIFUL DARK PAPERS THOUGH, WHICH I BROUGHT WITH ME WHEN I MOVED TO BERKS FOR GRAD SCHOOL, AND MY CHALKS AND CONTE CRAYONS. MY SECRET SUPER POWER IS THAT I WAS AN ART MAJOR BEFORE I WANDERED OFF INTO PHYSICS RESEARCH LET ME KNOW IF YOU WANT TO DO A PORTRAIT EXCHANGE SOMETIME. —VIOLET

INSTANTLY SMITTEN

WOW.

I SAID YES, LET'S MEET.

BEFORE MEETING HER I BLOW DRIED MY HAIR WITH A ROUND BRUSH.

much effort.

I SAW THAT "COLOR" AND "PATTERN" WERE THINGS SHE LISTED UNDER "SIX THINGS I COULDN'T LIVE WITHOUT," SO I WORE MY TURQUOISE DRESS WITH A SCARF WITH BLUE CIRCLES AND NAVY TIGHTS.

GOOD JOB

heels

SHE SAW THAT I'D LISTED "EUCALYPTUS" AND "LIGHT" IN THE SAME SECTION, SO SHE SUGGESTED WE MEET IN A EUCALYPTUS GROVE TWO BLOCKS FROM MY OFFICE. I HADN'T KNOWN IT EVEN EXISTED.

WHEN I GOT THERE, SHE WAS SITTING ON A LOG WEARING A PLAID SHIRT OVER A STRIPED SHIRT, AND HOLDING A TOOL BOX, FULL OF ARTSY UTENSILS SHE HAD MADE HERSELF...

HI, I'M VIOLET.

...LIKE A FEATHERY BRUSH FOR BLENDING...

...AND A SHARPENED STICK FOR A QUILL.

I DREW HER FIRST...

...SHE HAD POINTY EARS LIKE AN ELF AND A VERY THIN THROAT.

THANKS--SO FAST!

SHE TOOK HER TIME DRAWING ME - WITH HER CONTE CRAYONS AND FEATHER-BRUSH AND DARK EVERGREEN PAPER. WE TALKED ABOUT SCIENCE.

SO... YOU STUDY PHYSICS?

I DID AS AN UNDERGRAD BUT NOW I STUDY THE NORTHERN LIGHTS.

WOW. HAVE YOU SEEN THE AURORA?

ONLY ONCE... IN UPSTATE MICHIGAN. I'M WORKING ON A TELESCOPE TO SEE IT BETTER AND THEN I'M GOING TO ANTARCTICA NEXT YEAR.

HOW EXCITING! THE ONLY THING I REMEMBER ABOUT SCIENCE IS EXPLOSIONS.

EXPLOSIONS ARE PROBABLY THE BEST WAY TO SEDUCE PEOPLE INTO SCIENCE- I THINK STELLAR EVOLUTION WAS WHAT HOOKED ME, STARS BLOWING UP...

I REALLY, REALLY LOVED MY HIGH SCHOOL GEOLOGY CLASS- BECAUSE I LIKE MOUNTAINS AND ROCKS

THE ONLY ROCK I REMEMBER IS HEMA-TITE BECAUSE OF HOW SURPRIZINGLY HEAVY IT FEELS FOR ITS SIZE.

I LIKE MALACHITE... OBSIDIAN... SERPENTINE, OH, AND ULEXITE.

IT WAS BOTH WEIRD AND FLATTERING TO BE THE ONE BEING DRAWN. I WONDER IF I WAS GRINNING NERVOUSLY AND BLINKING LESS OFTEN THAN IS NATURAL, LIKE MANY OF THE WOMEN I DRAW DO.

I CONFESS-- UNTIL RECENTLY I THOUGHT PHILLIP PULLMAN MADE UP THE AURORA FOR THE GOLDEN COMPASS BOOKS.

HA! NO. IT'S REAL... AND IT'S MAGICAL.

SHE GAVE ME MY POR-
TRAIT, WHICH WAS VERY
DETAILED AND COLORFUL.

YOU MADE MY
EYES GREEN.

THEY *ARE* GREEN
IN THIS LIGHT.

SHE SUGGESTED WE GO
EAT SOMEWHERE FOR TEA
AND I SAID YES, EVEN
THOUGH IT SEEMED LIKE A
WASTE OF TIME AND MONEY
BECAUSE CLEARLY WE SHOULD
JUST GET *MARRIED*.

I WONDERED IF MAYBE THE OKCUPID ALGORITHM
ACTUALLY *WORKS*; IT HAD TOLD ME WE WERE A
95% MATCH, AND HERE WE WERE, GETTING ALONG.

AU COQUELET

PASTRIES 2000 ESPRESSO

THIS PLACE IS
MY FAVORITE.

VIOLET PAID FOR MY
DIGS— A WHITE HOT
CHOCOLATE AND A
FRUIT TART.

I WISH IT WOULD RAIN. THE SMELL OF SOIL AND PLANTS BECOMES MUCH STRONGER. BUT EARL GREY WILL DO, IN THE MEANTIME...

YEAH I LIKE THE ARID CALIFORNIA BRUSH-SMELLS.

I LIKE LATE AUTUMN THE BEST, WHEN IT STARTS TO GET COOLER.

THE BEST SMELL EVER IS THE *EVENING* AFTER A RAIN, IN THE LATE SPRING WHEN CHERRY BLOSSOMS ARE BLOOMING.

OOH LILAC. MY MOM LOVES LILAC SMELL.

YEAH IN MINNESOTA THE WINTER CAN REALLY TEST YOUR PATIENCE... SO THE SPRING IS SO MAGICAL... CHERRY AND THEN LILAC AND THEN APPLE BLOSSOMS.

OH, I HAD A GALLERY EVENT ON THURSDAY! I MADE A DRAWING OF DEATH VALLEY, AND, PEOPLE LOOKED AT IT...

THAT'S SO COOL. I'VE NEVER BEEN TO A CAPITAL-D-DESERT.

SO... HOW'S OK CUPID GOING FOR YOU? YOUR PROFILE IS SO CLEVER, I BET YOU GET A TON OF RESPONSE.

HA! NO. I'VE BEEN ON A FEW ONLINE DATES...

THE THING ABOUT OKCUPID LESBIANS IS THEY ALL WANT BABIES. LIKE...EW.

HUH?

NOT THAT THIS SHOULD EVEN BE A FIRST DATE ISSUE, BUT WANTING BABIES WAS WHY I BROKE UP WITH JAMES. SO... SHIT.

I GUESS THAT'S WHERE THE OTHER 5% WENT.

silence

OH... IS HAVING KIDS SOMETHING THAT'S *IMPORTANT* TO YOU?

OBVIOUSLY NOT RIGHT *NOW.* BUT, YES...

FOUR MINUTES LATER:

BERKELEY

ALRIGHT, SEE YOU.

YEAH... CALL ME.

SHE SENT ME A PRETTY NICE TEXT:

I ENJOYED MEETING YOU. YOU HAVE AN ABUNDANCE OF TALENT, A GOOD HEART, AND BEAUTIFUL EYES (WHICH, IN MY OPINION, CHANGE COLOR DEPENDING ON THE ANGLE.) IN FAIRNESS THOUGH, I FEEL I SHOULD SAY THAT I CAN'T HELP BEING VERY AWARE OF THE DIFFERENCE IN OUR AGES, AND I WOULD NOT FEEL COMFORTABLE WITH US GOING BEYOND FRIENDSHIP. I WOULD BE HAPPY TO HANG OUT AGAIN IF YOU WOULD STILL LIKE TO, BUT I FEEL IT'S IMPORTANT TO BE HONEST. YOU DESERVE SOMETHING WONDERFUL, I HOPE YOU FIND IT SOON.

SIGH...

CHRIS

MARCH 19, 2014

Choose your own adventure!

I'D SET IT UP THIS WAY BECAUSE I WAS VERY EXCITED ABOUT MEETING THE WOMAN—A PHOTO-JOURNALIST FROM DC WHO HAD JUST BEEN FEATURED AT A GALLERY IN OAKLAND.

I TEND TO GET REALLY INTO PEOPLE I LIKE TOO QUICKLY, AND SINCE I WAS SINGLE FOR THE FIRST TIME SINCE I WAS SEVENTEEN, WHY NOT MEET AS MANY PEOPLE AS POSSIBLE?

HIS NAME WAS CHRIS AND HE WAS REALLY INTO SCI-FI. I PREFER "FANTASY" BUT I APPRECIATE NERDS IN GENERAL.

HE ALSO APPARENTLY LIKED TO BAKE SWEETS, WHICH PIQUED MY INTEREST, OBV.

I can cook! I can make eclairs from scratch!

AW...

HE PICKED ME UP IN A REALLY NICE CAR...

...AND WE WENT TO GET JAPANESE FOOD.

WE TALKED FOR A FRUSTRATINGLY LONG TIME-- WELL AFTER I HAD FINISHED EATING MY STALE SUSHI. AT ONE POINT HE WAS TELLING ME IN DETAIL ABOUT WHY HE LOVED A SCIFI WRITER I HAD NEVER HEARD OF.

I THINK THE ROBOTS IN HER BOOKS SEEM HAPPIER THAN THE PEOPLE...

YEAH, PEOPLE ARE PRETTY MISERABLE.

He was pretty

MAYBE IF WE COULD BE *ALONE* TOGETHER...

WANT TO GO FOR A WALK?

OKAY.

33

AS IT TURNED OUT, HE WAS AN EXTREMELY AGREEABLE GUY.

WANT TO SIT ON THIS BENCH?

OKAY.

WANT TO MAKE OUT?

OKAY.

MAYBE WE SHOULD GO BACK TO YOUR CAR?

SURE.

PROBABLY THE BACK SEAT WOULD BE MORE COMFORTABLE ...

YEAH.

ONCE WE WERE IN THE BACK WE WERE HAVING A PRETTY GOOD GO AT IT. I KEPT WANTING THINGS TO HEAT UP MORE, OR GO JUST A BIT FURTHER...

...AND THEN THINGS WERE PERFECT FOR ABOUT THIRTY SECONDS, AND THEN HE MADE SOME SMALL JERK THAT I HADN'T EXPECTED, AND FOR SOME REASON...

AND SUDDENLY...

I PANICKED. I FROZE UP, SHUT DOWN, AND WENT AWAY. HE WAS CONFUSED AND ALARMED AND KEPT ASKING IF HE HAD DONE SOMETHING WRONG, BUT I COULDN'T THINK OF HOW TO EXPLAIN.

FINALLY I WAS ABLE TO SAY, TO THE WINDOW, THAT I JUST REALLY NEEDED TO GO HOME.

HE DROVE ME TO THE BART AND ASKED IF I WANTED HIM TO WAIT WITH ME FOR THE TRAIN.

NO. SORRY. THANK YOU. BYE.

THE NEXT MORNING HE TEXTED ME:

Hey are you ok? You seemed sad last night.

Yes I'm okay thankyou

IT TURNED OUT, HE WAS A VERY KIND PERSON.

BUT I NEVER SAW HIM AGAIN.

GRETCHEN

MAR 20, 2014

I CONSIDERED CANCELL-ING MY DATE THE NEXT DAY BECAUSE OF MY SURPRISINGLY TRIGGERED REACTION TO CHRIS...

WTF?

BUT INSTINCT TOLD ME GRETCHEN WASN'T THE KIND OF WOMAN WHO COMES ALONG EVERY DAY. SO I PULLED MYSELF TOGETHER.

SEE YOU THIS EVENING.

WE HAD BEEN PLANNING ON GOING TO SEE AN ARGENTINIAN PUNK BAND, BUT THE DETAILS OF THAT EVENT WENT UNDERGROUND AT THE LAST MINUTE, SO WE WENT TO VENUS CAFE.

I'VE NEVER BEEN HERE.

IT'S GOOD.

I NOTICED WHILE SHE HELD HER MENU THAT HER HANDS WERE LARGE AND GRACEFUL.

SHE HAD SAID ON HER PROFILE THAT THE "FIRST THING PEOPLE USUALLY NOTICE "ABOUT HER IS HER VOICE...

hm... LET'S SEE...

... AND IT WAS, INDEED, ENCHANTING. LOW AND BOTH CLEAR AND HUSKY, LIKE TWO VOICES THAT HAVE BEEN EDITED TOGETHER.

I THINK I'LL HAVE THE KALE SALAD.

venus

...WOAH, SELF. THIS IS A BIT EARLY FOR FEELING SO CRUSHY, EVEN FOR YOU.

SHE LOOKED AT MY SKETCHBOOK, AND SHE DIDN'T JUST SAY "YOU'RE SO GOOD" LIKE MOST PEOPLE -- SHE ASKED THOUGHTFUL, SMART QUESTIONS, AND TALKED SOME ABOUT HER PHOTOGRAPHY.

DO YOU ALWAYS WORK IN BLACK AND WHITE, OR DO YOU ADD COLOR?

ARE PEOPLE YOUR FAVORITE TO DRAW?

I LIKE PHOTO-GRAPHING PORTRAITS

ARE YOU GOING TO PUBLISH YOUR COMICS? OR MAKE A BOOK?

ARE ALL THESE PEOPLE REALLY THIS BEAUTIFUL AND REGAL, OR DO YOU DRAW THEM PRETTIER THAN THEY REALLY ARE?

WHY DO YOU DRAW SO LARGE?

DO YOU DRAW EVERY DAY? HOW QUICKLY DO YOU GO THROUGH BOOKS?

IT WAS COOL THAT SHE SEEMED SO ENGAGED...

WHO WOULD YOU SAY IS THE ARTIST WORKING CURRENTLY WHO INSPIRES YOU MOST DIRECTLY?

UM...JULIA WERTZ? WHO WROTE "THE INFINITE WAIT."

I'LL HAVE TO CHECK HER OUT.

AFTER DINNER I DREW HER ON THE BART TRAIN. SHE HAD BEAUTIFUL ANGLES.

YOU HAVE BEAU-TIFUL ANGLES.

SO QUICKLY, I'D GONE FROM ALMOST CANCELLING OUR MEETING TO WONDERING HOW LONG IT WAS SOCIALLY GRACEFUL TO WAIT BEFORE TEXTING HER.

SHE WOUND UP TEXTING ME ON FRIDAY TO SAY SHE WANTED TO HANG OUT AGAIN.

WE WENT TO SEE THE GRAND BUDAPEST HOTEL AT THE CALIFORNIA THEATRE ON KITTREDGE.

IT WAS A VERY FUNNY MOVIE WITH STELLAR ART DIRECTION AND CAST...

TILDA SWINTON

BUT I WAS MORE INTERESTED IN LOOKING AT GRETCHEN AND SEEING HER FACE IN THE BLUE LIGHT OF THE SCREEN, SEEING HOW IT CHANGED WHEN SHE LAUGHED OR WAS BORED OR WAS CURIOUS.

POP

I DIDN'T KNOW IF I SHOULD TRY TO HOLD HER HAND...

CORN

...SO I JUST KEPT MY HAND VISIBLY PLACED BETWEEN US.

AFTER THE MOVIE I GAVE HER SOME THINGS...

HERE ARE THOSE WRITER CARDS I'VE BEEN WORKING ON...

EMILY DICKINSON

AAH... BEAUTIFUL!

AND HERE'S *THE INFINATE WAIT*, THAT JULIA WERTZ BOOK.

THE INFINITE WAIT

HAHA, YOU'RE GONNA LAUGH WHEN YOU SEE WHAT I BROUGHT YOU.

IT WAS AN ORIGINAL, SIGNED DRAWING BY JULIA WERTZ, OF ONE OF THE *INFINITE WAIT* PANELS. I COULDN'T BELIEVE IT.

THERE'S NOTHING FOR ME OUT THERE

OH MY GOD... HOW???

J. Wertz

OH I JUST ORDERED HER BOOK ONLINE AND THERE WAS THE OPTION TO PAY A LITTLE EXTRA FOR A DRAWING... SO...

IT'S THE SORT OF THING *I* USUALLY TRY TO PULL OFF FOR PEOPLE I LIKE...

I LOVE IT!

...SO TO BE ON THE RECEIVING END OF SUCH A GIFT WAS WONDERFUL.

THANK YOU.

YOU'RE WELCOME ... IT WAS NO BIG TROUBLE ...

LATER, WITH MY BEST BUDDY TINA:

HAVE YOU EVER GONE OUT WITH A GUY A FEW TIMES AND NOT KNOWN IF HE WAS INTO YOU ROMANTICALLY OR JUST AS A FRIEND?

mmm...

NO, ACTUALLY.

WHAT'S *THAT* LIKE?

WELL IT WAS A SECOND DATE AND WE EXCHANGED GIFTS, BUT WE NEVER KISSED OR HELD HANDS.

BUT MAYBE WE'RE BOTH WAITING FOR THE OTHER PERSON TO MAKE THE FIRST MOVE?

MAYBE. AND ...SOUNDS LIKE YOU REALLY LIKE HER?

YEAH! SHE'S SMART AND HAS A SEXY VOICE... AND SHE IS VERY BEAUTIFUL, IT'S ALMOST RIDICULOUS...

SOUNDS LIKE YOU SHOULD JUST *ASK* HOW SHE FEELS NEXT TIME?

DOOO IT!

YEAH, I GUESS...

YOU CAN *DO IT!* AND THEN TELL ME EVERYTHING!

MAYBE YOU'LL GET MARRIED!

GRETCHEN SUGGESTED WE MEET FOR DRINK & DRAW NIGHT AT THE NEW PARKWAY. WE GOT THERE EARLY SO WE COULD CHAT.

WORK! TRAVEL EXE?

ART!

podcasts!

PHOTOGRAPHY!

childhood

I BROUGHT HER A COPY OF THE "BLUE IS THE WARMEST COLOR" GRAPHIC NOVEL TO SUGGEST A TONE...

IT'S MUCH BETTER THAN THE MOVIE.

COOL!

SHE SHOWED ME THE PHOTOGRAPHY PROJECT SHE WAS WORKING ON, PORTRAITS OF FIRST GENERATION IMMIGRANTS LIVING IN SAN FRANCISCO, WHICH WOULD RUN ALONG SIDE A STORY IN THE SF CHRONICLE.

THE PHOTOS MADE ME WANT TO ADD MORE LIGHT AND SHADOW TO MY OWN DRAWINGS OF PEOPLE.

HEY...I'M GONNA BE DRAWING PORTRAITS AT PEGASUS BOOKS FOR THEIR BOOK FAIR DAY. DO YOU WANT TO COME TOO, AND LIKE, PHOTOGRAPH PEOPLE?

YEAH! IT'LL BE COOL TO PUT THEM TOGETHER SIDE BY SIDE.

WE COULD WRITE DOWN THEIR STORIES, TOO, AND MAKE A BLOG!

WHEN THE DRINK-AND-DRAW STARTED I REALIZED HOW SUCCESSFUL GRETCHEN WAS—SEVERAL OF THE ARTISTS AT THE TABLE KNEW HER WORK. AND THROUGH A COMBINATION OF HER CHARISMA AND HER UNUSUAL VOICE, SHE BECAME THE PERSON AT THE TABLE WHO OTHER PEOPLE WANTED TO GET TO KNOW.

chatter chatter chatter   chatter chatter chatter   chatter chatter

SHE EVEN HAD A NATURAL FLAIR FOR DRAWING, WITH AN ELEGANT LINE.

woah...you're good.   thanks.

WATCHING HER CHARM EVERYONE, I COULDN'T HELP COMPARING HER TO JAMES, WHO WAS SO SHY AROUND MY FAMILY AND FRIENDS. IT MIGHT BE NICE TO HAVE SUCH AN EXTROVERTED PLUS ONE AT THANKSGIVING.

ON OUR WAY BACK TO THE BART STATION, I WAS THINKING:

Ask her TELL her kiss her SOMETHING STEP IT UP

ACCORDING TO THE SIGN, I HAD THREE MINUTES IF I WANTED TO BROACH THE SUBJECT TONIGHT.

PTS BAY POINT 3 MIN
10 CAR TRAIN

SO...

...YES?

UM, CAN I KISS YOU? IS THAT A THING?

I DON'T KNOW...

I REALLY JUST-- REALLY WANT TO BE YOUR FRIEND.

I THINK YOU'RE AMAZING AND I DO STILL REALLY WANT TO COLLABORATE WITH YOU ON THAT BLOG BUT I JUST-- OK CUPID DATING IS SO FAST AND SO "YES OR NO" SO SUDDENLY, CAN WE JUST BE FRIENDS AND PRETEND WE MET AT A PARTY?

OKAY.

I'M SORRY... I HOPE I DIDN'T LEAD YOU ON...

IT'S FINE. THIS IS MY TRAIN.

43

AFTER A FEW DAYS OF SADNESS AND SELF PITY I THOUGHT I WAS DUE...

melancholy

SAD PLAYLIST

...AND SOME CIRCLES OF SELF-DOUBT...

...BUT WE GOT ALONG SO WELL. IT MUST BE THAT I'M NOT THIN OR PRETTY ENOUGH...

BAJA FRESH

(I THINK WHILE EATING AN ENORMOUS COMFORT-BURRITO)

...AND SOME DRINKS WITH FRIENDS...

AWW. SORRY GIRL.

NO, IT'S FINE...

...I REALIZED THAT FINDING A KIND, CREATIVE FRIEND FROM ONLINE IS STILL A HUGE WIN. WE DID THE COLLABORATION AT PEGASUS BOOKS...

CREATIVE

DOUBLE ACT!!!

...AND WHEN I WAS WORKING ON AN ANIMATION, SHE DID A VOICE OVER FOR IT.

TAKE ONE

SHE COMES TO CHEER ME ON WHEN I DO COMICS READINGS OR ZINEFESTS...

THESE LOOK GREAT!

...AND I CALL HER UP TO CONGRATULATE HER WHEN HER SHOTS RUN IN PAPERS OR MAGAZINES.

AMAZING!

HAVING A FRIEND WHO IS ALSO AN ARTIST--BOTH NATURALLY TALENTED AND SKILLED AND HARD WORKING-IS GREAT.

ARTIST SYNERGY

JESSICA

MAY 28, 2014

JESSICA SAW ON MY PROFILE THAT I (USED TO) SPEAK SOME JAPANESE AND ASKED ME ON A SUSHI DATE AT KIJI RESTAURANT. I HAD BEEN IGNORING OKCUPID BUT I SPONTANEOUSLY ACCEPTED.

HI.

HI.

IN OUR BRIEF CHAT ONLINE WE NOTED OUR MATCHY HAIR AND GLASSES. IN THE MIRROR BEHIND HER I NOTICED HOW MUCH WEIGHT I'D GAINED SINCE JANUARY.

I MOVED FOR WORK, AND TO GET OUT OF AUGUSTA.

AS IF TO UNDERLINE THIS FACT, OUR EXPENSIVE SUSHI CAME OUT IN TINY PORTIONS...

WTF IS THIS??

I WAS STARVING, BUT I TRIED TO FOCUS ON THE CONVERSATION...

SO... WHAT'S THE NEW JOB?

I'LL BE A "MESSAGE INTELLIGENCE PROJECT MANAGER" AT YELP.

OH, COOL! WHAT IS A...

"MESSAGE INTELLIGENCE OFFICER"... IT SOUNDS CREEPIER THAN IT IS. IT'S AN ENGINEERING GIG TO HELP MAKE THEIR ADS MORE RELEVANT.

SO... DO YOU KNOW A LOT OF MATH?

I MEAN, YEAH MY DEGREE IS IN ENGINEERING.

I'M ACTUALLY HOPING TO MOVE MORE INTO THE DESIGN SIDE OF THE BUSINESS...

...BUT IT'S GREAT TO BE HERE IN THE BAY. YELP HAS EXCELLENT TRANS-INCLUSIVE HEALTHCARE AND IT'LL BE AWESOME TO BE OUT AT WORK.

YELP IS SO GREAT IN SF, SO MANY PLACES!

YESTERDAY I WENT TO THIS TEA GARDEN WITH ANOTHER GIRL...

...IT WAS ALSO RATED HIGHLY...

...ACTUALLY I SHOULD REALLY GO BECAUSE MY DATE from YESTERDAY IS AT MY APARTMENT. I PROBABLY SHOULDN'T HAVE COME TONIGHT, BUT I WANTED TO TRY THE SUSHI!

WELL... GOOD LUCK AT YOUR NEW JOB.

THANKS!

MICHAEL

JULY 31, 2014

I WOKE UP ONE DAY IN LATE JULY AND IT WAS HOOK-UP-O'CLOCK.

AS IN RIGHT NOW!

SO I CHANGED MY OK CUPID SETTINGS TO "INTERESTED IN MEN", AND FIRED OFF MESSEGES TO A DOZEN GUYS. BECAUSE...THEY'RE EASIER.

Want to hang out?

want to hang out?

want to hang out?

want to hang out?

I ARRANGED TO MEET A GUY NAMED MICHAEL THAT SAME EVENING.

cat's in the cradle...

I GOT MODERATELY DOLLED UP BUT HAD TO RUSH TO WORK...

OVER LUNCH:

I DON'T WANT ANOTHER CAR-GUY DEBACLE...BUT...MAKING OUT IS GOOD.

MAKING OUT IS VERY GOOD.

TOSS NOODLE BAR

IT WAS TO BE *YET ANOTHER* SUSHI DATE, BUT I CHOSE THE PLACE THIS TIME -- *NANAYIRO*, ON SHATTUCK.

THEY SERVE HUGE HELPINGS OF GREAT FOOD FOR A REASONABLE PRICE. (WRITE THIS DOWN, KIDS!)

BUT ALAS, WHEN MICHAEL SHOWED UP, I WASN'T ATTRACTED TO HIM. AT ALL. HE'D LOOKED CUTE IN HIS PICTURE BUT IN PERSON HE LOOKED LIKE A KID IN HIS DAD'S SUIT.

HI! ELIZABETH?

THERE WAS NOTHING FOR IT BUT TO JUST EAT DINNER

HOW WAS YOUR DAY?

STRESSFUL. I HAD A JOB INTERVIEW AND NO MONEY SO I HAD TO BORROW MY DAD'S SUIT.

I'M SUCH A JERK.

I WISHED I COULD STAND UP AND SAY:

I'M SO SORRY, BUT I WAS *ACTUALLY* JUST MEETING YOU BECAUSE I WAS HOPING TO USE YOUR BODY FOR ~~SEX~~ SOME SECOND BASE ACTION... BUT NOW THAT I'VE MET YOU, I THINK I'D ACTU-ALLY RATHER EAT MY SUSHI ALONE, SO COULD YOU PLEASE, LIKE, SKEDADDLE?

THANKFULLY, I DID NOT DO THIS. WE CHATTED AND HE WAS REASONABLY INTERESTING.

SO... WHERE WAS YOUR INTERVIEW?

AT ALTERNET, AN ALTERNATIVE PUBLICATION.

OH, I KNOW ~~RNET.~~

YEAH IT'S A JOURNALISM JOB.

I LOVE WRITING.

I WAS EVEN START-ING TO RECONSIDER WHETHER THIS DATE WAS A DUD WHEN:

MY BAND JUST FIN-ISHED OUR FIRST EP. WANT TO HEAR IT?

CRASH BANG CLANG Grrrr ROAR DRUM GRR BANG

IT WAS SOME SORT OF GARAGE-METAL.

LET ME BE CLEAR: IT SOUNDED *TERRIBLE.*

IT SOUNDS GREAT!

LET'S GET THE CHECK...

MALLORY AND BEN

AUGUST 17, 2014

A FEW WEEKS LATER, A COUPLE ASKED ME IF I WANTED TO "GET TO KNOW THEM" BEFORE THEY WENT TO BURNING MAN. I HAD A MINUTE OF INDIGNATION ABOUT HOW BISEXUALS ALWAYS GET THREESOME REQUESTS...

...AND THEN I RESPONDED "YES." THEY WERE HOT. I SUGGESTED WE MEET AT THE LEXINGTON CLUB THE NEXT EVENING.

WHEN THEY SHOWED UP, MALLORY AND BEN WERE STUNNING-- PHYSICALLY. IN TERMS OF CONVERSATION THEY WERE PRETTY BANAL. SO I DREW THEM AND ASKED ABOUT THEIR BURNING MAN PLANS.

WE DON'T REALLY PLAN FOR IT.

IT'S FUN TO JUST SHOW UP AND SEE WHO YOU MEET.

IT'S A FREE FOR ALL.

THEY WERE LATE. I DREW THE CUTE BARTENDER AND ORDERED A BLUE MOON.

ONCE I GAVE THEM THEIR DRAWING, THEY ABRUPTLY LEFT.

here you g--

K THX BYE!

I WAS CONFUSED.

WTF?

THEN I REMEMBERED THAT I HADN'T CHANGED MY PROFILE PICTURE SINCE I SIGNED UP IN JANUARY, AND... HM.

HOW I LOOKED IN JANUARY...

HOW I LOOKED ON THIS DATE...

HOW I FELT AT THIS PARTICULAR MOMENT...

I DRANK MY BEER, FEELING AS DESIREABLE AS MOLD -- OR, INDEED, AS MICHAEL.

OH WELL.

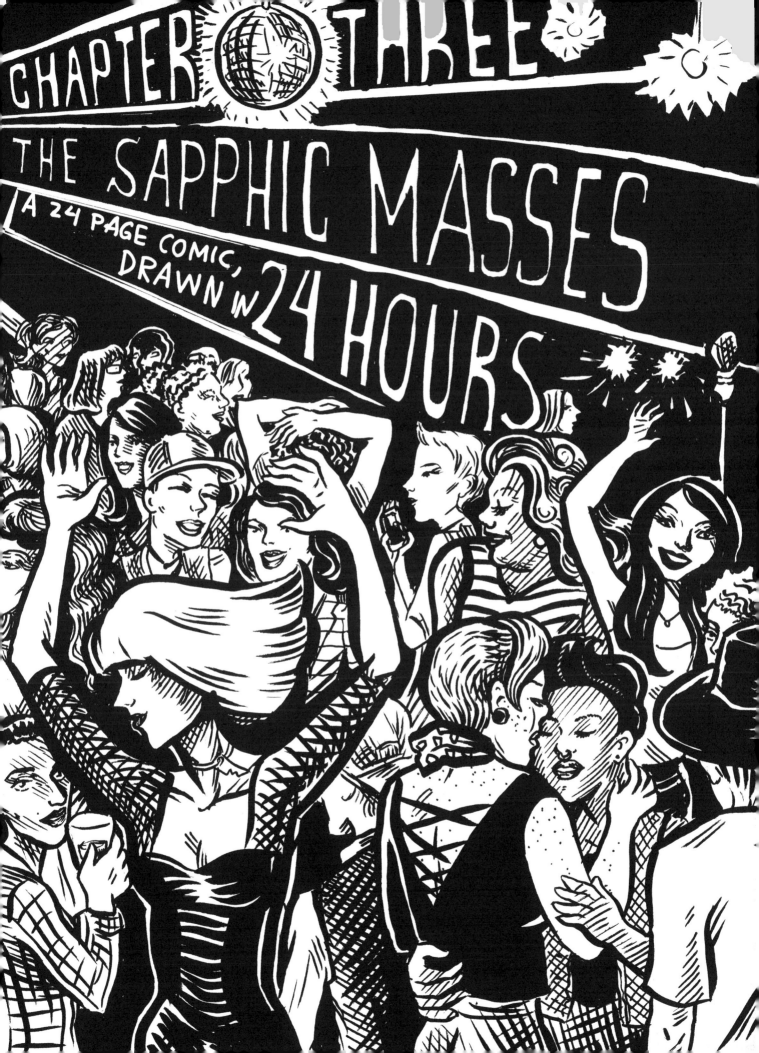

THE SAPPHIC MASSES

A 24 HOUR COMIC BY ELIZABETH BEIER egbeier.tumblr

♪ PART ONE ♪

SO SEXY ALL CAPS

IT WAS A DARK AND STORMY NIGHT.

ummm yes.

AS IN: DARK RUM, GINGER BEER & LIME.

IT WAS FRIDAY SEPT 12, 2014. ON TUESDAY I HAD BEEN HAVING A MOMENT...

HOLY SHIT EVERYTHING is CHANGING so FAST...

MUST DO SOMETHING DRASTIC!!!

SO I CUT OFF MY HAIR !!!

WELL, A NICE LADY NAMED PAM AT "WORLD CUTS" DID.

WHAT DO YOU THINK

WOAH. I...

FUCKING LOVE IT!

ABOUT A YEAR AGO I HAD BEEN MUCH THINNER AND HAD CUT MY HAIR INTO A BOB LIKE MEGAN FROM *mad men...*

SO FLY...

BUT IT HADN'T BEEN THAT SITUATION IN A WHILE. MY HAIR HAD BEEN MORE LIKE AN ACCIDENT HAPPENING ALL OVER MY FACE.

meh.

I WALKED OUT OF WORLD CUTS ON A CLOUD OF SWAGGERING BAD-ASSERY.

I WENT TO PARIS BAGUETTE WHERE I KNOW THERE IS GOOD LIGHTING TO TAKE A SELFIE FOR FACEBOOK

AND THE RESPONSE WAS SWIFT AND AFFIRMING.

MY EX BOYFRIEND EMAILED ME JUST: "You are about to get so much pussy."

AND THIS SCORCHINGLY GORGEOUS WOMAN I'M FRIENDS WITH TEXTED FIVE TIMES TO SAY:

you look amazing

OMG

WOW

WOW WOW WOW

SO SEXY MUCH STYLE SUCH QUEER

SO SEXY ALL CAPS, HUH?...

SO FOR THE REST OF THE WEEK I WAS DYING FOR THE WEEKEND WHEN I COULD GO OUT AND HOPEFULLY, ACTUALLY FACTUALLY, FINALLY HOOK UP WITH A WOMAN.

AAAAH WHY IS NOT FRIDAY

WHERE SHOULD I GO FOR GIRLS

SO SEXY ALL CAPS

GIRLS GIRLS GIRLS

AAAAH

GIRLS GIRLS GIRLS

I DIDN'T WANT TO GO TO THE LEX AGAIN BECAUSE THERE'S NO ACTION THERE AND I WAS ALWAYS LIKE:

SIT IN CORNER, DRAW, STARE HUNGRILY AT HOTTIES PLAYING POOL

AND I WANTED TO BE LIKE:

DANCE WITH GIRLS—HEY GIRL

I DECIDED TO GO TO THE WHITE HORSE BECAUSE INTERNET SAID THERE WAS DANCING ON FRIDAYS...

white horse

GIRLS GIRLS GIRLS GIRLS

BUT BECAUSE I WENT THERE STRAIGHT AFTER WORK LIKE A (HORNY) DOOFUS THERE WERE ONLY LIKE SIX PEOPLE THERE.

GI...UH...

AND I WAS DEFINITELY THE ONLY ONE UNDER AGE FORTY.

57

I DECIDED TO JUST DRAW THE ELDER QUEERS...

well sweetie...

...IN EXCHANGE FOR THEIR STORIES. WHILE DRINKING DARK AND STORMIES. IT WAS AWESOME.

Heidi

well I can honestly say I'm at my happiest NOW...

Because I SPENT my life doing construction work...

and I took the train so I had to get up at like FIVE THIRTY...

which I HATED.

But now that I'm RETIRED I sleep until I wake up at eight... nine... even TEN!

AND I do whatever I WANT, like feeding MY CHICKENS...

I LOVE MY chickens. So yeah, life is good.

58

Curtis

I'VE BEEN COMING TO BARS SINCE I WAS YOUR AGE...

AND IT WAS A CRIME TO "IMPER-SONATE A MAN."...

...

(THEN SHE GOT LOST IN A MEMORY AND SHE DIDN'T CONTINUE.)

Rhonda

SO YEAH WHEN DID YOU KNOW YOU FAVOURED WOMEN?

OH, I HAD A FRIEND IN THIRD GRADE...

Oh GOD, I remember my fourth grade art teacher... Mrs. Carol... MRS CAROL!!

Heidi again:

heck, I knew from my SECOND GRAPEcrush

her name was JUNE and I was in LOVE with her & we walked home from SCHOOL together...

ONE DAY IT WAS RAINING so I put my umbrella over her and we were so close, I was thinking...

IS THIS OKAY?

THEIR STORIES DELIGHTED ME, BUT I STILL WANTED THE GIRLS GIRLS GIRLS, SO I WENT TO CHECK THE DANCE FLOOR...

GIRLS GIRLS GIRLS GIRLS GIRLS?

BUT THE ONLY PERSON THERE WAS AN ANCIENT MAN WHO WAS EITHER ASLEEP OR DEAD.

← HIS CANE

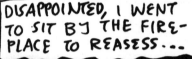

DISAPPOINTED, I WENT TO SIT BY THE FIRE-PLACE TO REASESS...

AND POST A DISGRUNTLED FACEBOOK STATUS...

THERE ARE NO GIRLS

h/t C. BURNS

BUT WHEN I LOOKED UP

THERE WAS HER.

60

IT TOOK MY DRUNK-BRAIN SEVERAL SECONDS TO REALIZE THAT THIS WAS **NOT** MY INCREDIBLY SEXY BUT RUTHLESSLY UNRELIABLE FRIEND FROM LA WHO HAD JUST RECENTLY BROKEN MY HEART...

nope...

...BUT AN ENTIRELY DIFFERENT HUMAN.

STILL... DAMN.

I SAID...

um, hi- cl see that you're watching... uh... SPORTS? but... can cl also, like, draw your face?

oh... and, cl'm Elizabeth.

SPORTS

uh... hii! and sure.

gul girl girl girl!

SO... WHAT GAME IS THIS, ANYWAY?

DODGERS VS. GIANTS.

SPORTS

WHICH IS... BASE-BALL?

... wait, really?

WE WOUND UP TALKING FOR OVER AN HOUR ABOUT WORK, DATING, SPORTS, AND ART, WHILE TRYING NOT TO GET HIT BY POOL CUES.

H/T ALEX ROBINSON.

AND THEN I WAS LIKE...

SO... I LIKE YOU.

AAAH SORRY THAT WAS OUTLOUD HUH, YOU SEEM COOL AND PRETTY AND SMART AND.. OH im just making this worse..

haha

IT'S OKAY. SO- AT WORK I'M A **LEADER** AND I GO FIRST AND SAY WHAT I MEAN, BUT IN THINGS LIKE THIS, I'M NOT LIKE THAT FOR SOME REASON.

OH *IN THAT CASE...*

WELL, IT LOOKS LIKE SOME PEOPLE ARE DANCING NOW... DO YOU WANT TO GO DO THAT?

OK.

SO I HID MY SKETCHBOOK AND WE APPROACHED THE FLOOR.

I'M A REALLY AWKWARD DANCER, BY THE WAY.

OH GOOD, ME TOO. IT'LL BE FINE.

SHE IS TALL

AND INDEED...

...AWKWARDNESS DID ENSUE.

I HAD ONLY ONCE ACHIEVED A STATE OF *DRUNKENNESS* SO COMPLETE THAT DANCING SEEMED FUN AND NOT VERY UNCOMFORTABLE...

IT WAS A FEW MONTHS EARLIER WITH MY COWORKERS AT A DETROIT NIGHTCLUB CALLED NIKKI'S LOUNGE. WE WERE THERE FOR A CONFERENCE CALLED NETROOTS NATION. I HAD MET ELIZABETH WARREN EARLIER THAT DAY.

heeeey... WOOHOO!!! DANCE! I AM BACCHUS!

UNFORTUNATELY FOR ME I WAS *NOT* NIKKI'S-LOUNGE-DRUNK NOW...

...BUT RATHER I FELT LIKE I WAS PLAYING A GAME OF TWISTER. (A GAME I HAD ALWAYS BEEN BAD AT.

IN FACT I WAS ONLY DANCING BECAUSE I HOPED IT WOULD LEAD TO MORE - FUN - MAKE-OUT-TIMES.

I DIDN'T KNOW WHAT TO DO WITH MY BODY.

WHEN I DANCED WITH GUYS IT WAS AT LEAST OBVIOUS HOW TO TURN THEM ON...

BUT I DIDN'T KNOW IF I DANCED WITH HER LIKE SHE WAS A DUDE, WOULD IT FEEL GOOD FOR HER? OR ME?

IS THIS HOW?

IT WAS NICE THAT SHE WAS TALLER AND WIDER THAN ME BECAUSE AT LEAST I FELT CUTE...

...WHICH HADN'T BEEN TRUE IN A WHILE...

BUT I DIDN'T KNOW SOME IMPORTANT THINGS

aaah

sorry!

LIKE: HOW HARD CAN I LEAN INTO HER WITHOUT KNOCKING US BOTH OVER?

WAS I ALLOWED TO TOUCH HER ANYWHERE OR JUST THE RESPECTFUL WAIST-AND-SHOULDER-AND-NECK-AREAS?

IF I WANTED HER TO KISS ME DID I HAVE TO TELL HER THIS WITH MY WORDS...

OR WOULD PSYCHIC EXHORTATIONS SUFFICE?

ON TOP OF ALL THIS I KEPT HAVING THOUGHTS SUCH AS:

oh god, I think I LOVE HER BUT I CAN'T TRUST HER

BEFORE REMEMBERING:

OH YEAH. DIFFERENT HUMAN!

SOME AMAZING THINGS HAPPENED. FOR INSTANCE, THE ANCIENT MAN WHO HAD BEEN SLEEPING WAS <u>TEARING UP</u> THE DANCE FLOOR...

WOAH.

OH!

dance!

AND LIKE, <u>REALLY</u> GETTING DOWN.

ALSO WE SAW THE "ANACONDA" VIDEO FOR THE FIRST TIME...

now is that even POSSIBLE?

...WOW...

WE BOTH STOOD AGASE.

"fuck these skinny Bitchez in the club

FINALLY SHE SAID...

Hey... do you wanna take a BREAK?

YA!

WE WENT OVER TO THE WINDO TO HAVE FRESH AIR AND WATCH PEOPLE PLAY BILLIARDS.

So yeah you see, he's putting a backspin. and now he gets to go again because he made it. he's looking just for the ones with the stripe... you see those, right?

I'M GOOD AT PETITIONS!

hey... IF I'm going back to my house on BART I should go pretty soon

HINT! HINT! HINT!

OH YEAH, I'LL DRIVE YOU TO THE BART.

I USED ALL MY BRAIN CONTROL POWERS...

kiss me dammit like really what are you waiting for just push me into this wall and you know what I DO WANT oh or we could go to your car car is good or you know somewhere else but mostly just I want you to kiss me at this point like now

DO YOU WANT TO GO NOW? OR... DO YOU NEED TO PEE OR SOMETHING!

SURE. I MEAN, THANKS.

IN THE CAR:

SO... YOU LIVE IN LAFAYETTE? WHY?

I LIVE WITH MY PARENTS.

OH. FUCK.

AT THE BART:

Well... here's your drawing... and my contact info... so...

THANKS. HAVE A SAFE RIDE HOME

ON THE BART RIDE HOME...

MAN WHY AM I GOING HOME BY MYSELF

MAYBE SHE WILL CALL. I DONT EVEN KNOW HER LAST NAME

ALTHOUGH HER FIRST NAME AND OCCUPATION IS ENOUGH TO FIND...

OH YEP. SHOULD I FRIEND ON FACEBOOK OR IS THAT TOO STALKERY.

I SHOULD HAVE AT THE LEAST SUGGESTED THAT WE MAKE OUT IN THE CAR

oh well...

the next morning.

NEED MORE CLUB GIRLS GIRLY GIRLS GIRLS GIRLS!

I MANICALLY CLEANED MY ROOM, WHICH HAD BEEN SQUALID FOR MONTHS, DURING THE DAY...

GIRLS GIRLS GIRLS GIRLS GIRLS GIRLS!

AND THAT EVENING I WENT TO A DANCE PARTY IN THE CITY THAT PROMISED WALL TO WALL LESBIANISM.

GIRLS GIRLS GIRLS GIRLS

68

PART TWO:

SOMEWHERE WITHIN THESE SAPPHIC MASSES

THE PARTY IS, REGRETABLY CALLED "COCKBLOCK." IT'S THE 2ND SATURDAY OF EVERY MONTH. I LEFT MY SKETCHBOOK AT HOME BECAUSE I SUSPECT THAT IT SEPARATES ME FROM PEOPLE.

I DRAW YOUR FACE AND THEN YOUR FACE IS NOT ON MY FACE IT IS ON MY DRAWING.

TONIGHT THE PLAN IS:

ZERO DRAWINGS, ALL BABES!

BUT IN MY EAGERNESS I ONCE AGAIN ARRIVED APPALLINGLY EARLY...

AND WAS REDUCED TO DRAWING ON NAPKINS.

THE CUTE BARTENDER...

aw, thanks!

THIS HOT WOMAN FROM UZBEKISTAN....

I'M JUST HERE BECAUSE MY FRIEND IS GETTING MARRIED IN A WEEK.

...AND HER FRIEND...

I'M DRUNK. REALLY DRUNK

EVENTUALLY THE DANCEFLOOR DID FILL UP, AND FOR SOME REASON... FEMMES WERE ALL OVER ME!

REALLY BEAUTIFUL WOMEN WERE TELLING ME STUFF LIKE...

BABE, you are SO organic and ambiguous!

...AND...

you are like... SOOOO WOMAN!

I DIDN'T KNOW WHAT TO MAKE OF THIS.

MEANWHILE THE WOMEN I WERE MOST ATTRACTED TO

TREATED ME WITH THE SAME INDIFFERENCE AS EVER.

BUT AT LEAST THIS DOESN'T HAPPEN ANYMORE...

UH, HI...

SORRY, I DON'T DANCE WITH STRAIGHT GIRLS.

A LOT OF THE ENERGY IN THE ROOM WAS NEAR THE STAGE, WHERE THERE WERE TWO DANCERS TAKING CASH AND TUCKING IT INTO THEIR LINGERIE.

SEEING THEM MADE ME FIRST SAD, THEN ENTHRALLED, THEN LIKE I REALLY SHOULD HAVE BROUGHT MY SKETCHBOOK. IT WAS _so_ SIN CITY.

I MADE NAPKIN DRAWINGS INSTEAD. IT REMINDED ME OF FIGURE DRAWING CLASSES...

EXCEPT FOR HOW THEY WERE WEARING CHAINS, AND UNDERWEAR, AND DOING STUFF LIKE THIS:

ANYHOW, THEY LIKED THEIR DRAWINGS...

OH MY GAWWD, SO SWEET!!

I'M GONNA TWEET THIS!!!

AND FRAME IT!

71

EVERY NOW AND THEN THE DANCING FELT AWKWARD AGAIN, BUT I HAD A SOLUTION. TO PARAPHRASE DORI THE FISH:

STILL— IT WAS FRUSTRATING TO BE AROUND SO MANY WOMEN BUT UNABLE TO TALK TO THEM. BECAUSE I WAS SURE THAT SOMEWHERE WITHIN THESE SAPPHIC MASSES THERE WERE BETWEEN THREE AND EIGHT PEOPLE I'D WANT TO DATE, AND MAYBE BETWEEN ONE AND THREE I COULD FALL IN LOVE WITH...

BUT IT WAS IMPOSSIBLE TO TELL WHICH ONES THEY WERE.

IT WAS ILLUMINATING TO SEE, UP CLOSE, WHAT SUCCESFUL LESBIAN DANCING WAS...

... SEEMS LIKE YOU HAVE TO UNDERSTAND RHYTHM.

PROBABLY THE COMPARATIVE ADVANTAGE IS FOR ME TO GO BACK TO DRAWING.

BECAUSE EVEN WITHOUT MY SKETCHBOOK, WHAT I BRING TO A SITUATION LIKE THIS IS MY POWER TO OBSERVE. I MIGHT GO BACK. THERE'S SOME CHARLES-BURNSY POTENTIAL TO THE MASSES.

AS THE EVENING BECAME NIGHT BECAME MORNING, PAIRS WERE GETTING MORE INTIMATE...

WHICH WAS STARTLING TO SEE SO CLOSE UP...

AND MADE ME FEEL A GHASTLY AMOUNT OF ENVY AND DESIRE FOR MY OWN SOMEONE.

EVEN THOUGH THE FEW TIMES I DID MAKE OUT WITH PEOPLE SINCE JAMES AND I BROKE UP...

(DRUNK, BEAUTIFUL BRAZILIAN GUY)...

OLÁ LINDA!

(SEXY PURPLE-HAIRED GIRL AT PRIDE)...

SURE, WHY NOT?

(FANCY CAR GUY FROM OK-CUPID....)

BACK SEAT?

(HIGH SCHOOL CRUSH REUNITED IN DETROIT.)

ELIZ-ABETH!

IT LEFT ME FEELING LONELIER THAN BEFORE.

UUU UUGHHH will be art HERMIT FOREVER

REMEMBERING THIS, I DECIDED TO GO HOME.

WHEN I WAS LITTLE MY FAVORITE PART OF GOING TO THE OCEAN WAS HOW IF I STOOD IN SHALLOW WATER...

THE WAVES ROLLING IN AND RECEDING MADE IT FEEL LIKE I WAS MOVING, EVEN THOUGH I WASN'T.

aaahaha

A SENSATION THAT SOMEHOW KEPT GOING UNTIL I WENT TO SLEEP.

...PERHAPS, MAGIC.

AFTER THESE CONSECUTIVE NIGHTS OF DANCING, I FELT SOMETHING SIMILAR, LIKE BEING STILL SURROUNDED BY MOVING BODIES...

WHICH WAS IRRITATING.

I WISHED THE ECHOES WOULD GO AWAY SO I COULD GO TO SLEEP.

I WANTED TO BE ALONE. BUT NOT ALONE.

SO I GUESS I DON'T KNOW WHAT I WANT.

EXCEPT THAT I DO.

I WANT...

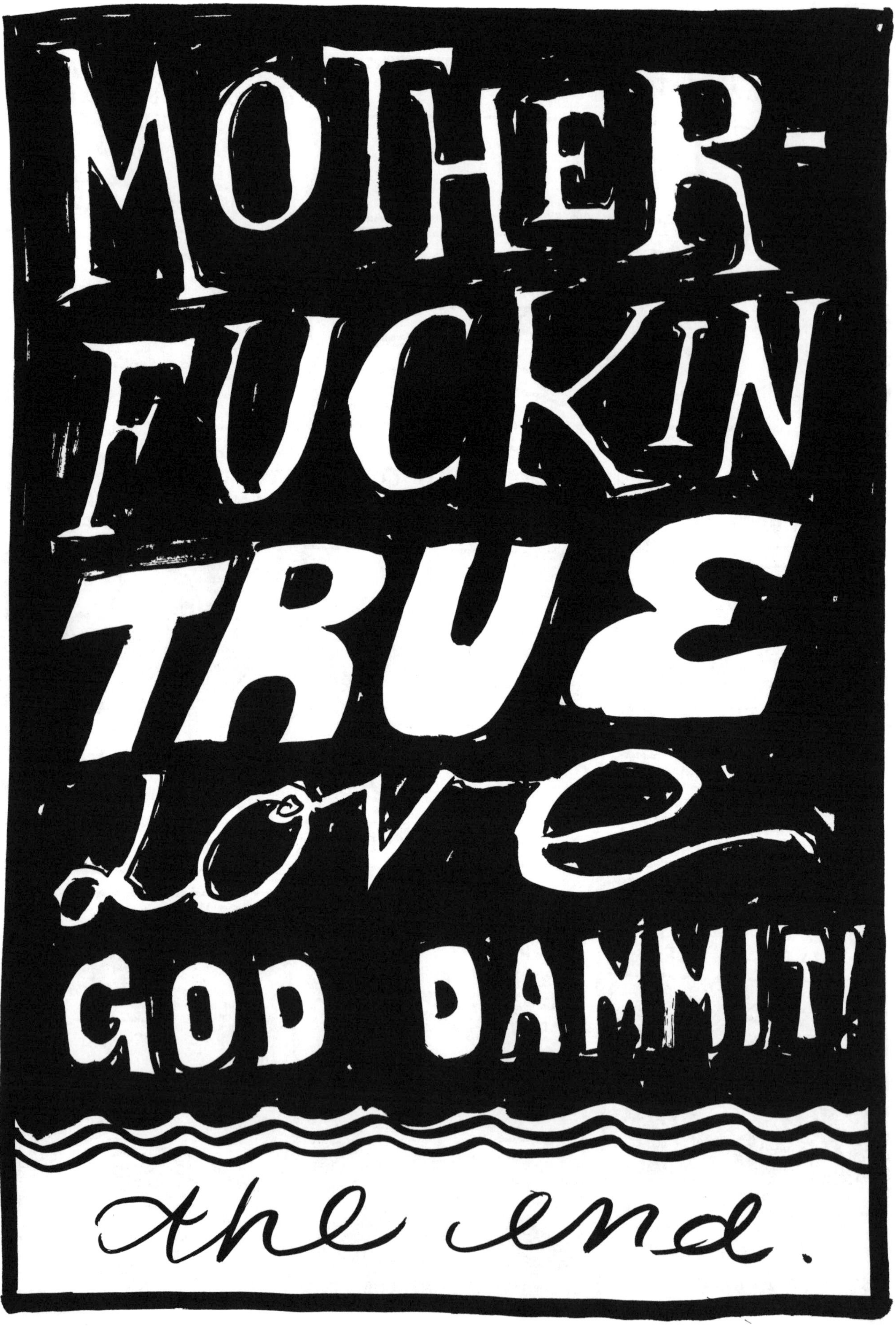
MOTHER-
FUCKIN
TRUE
love
GOD DAMMIT!
the end.

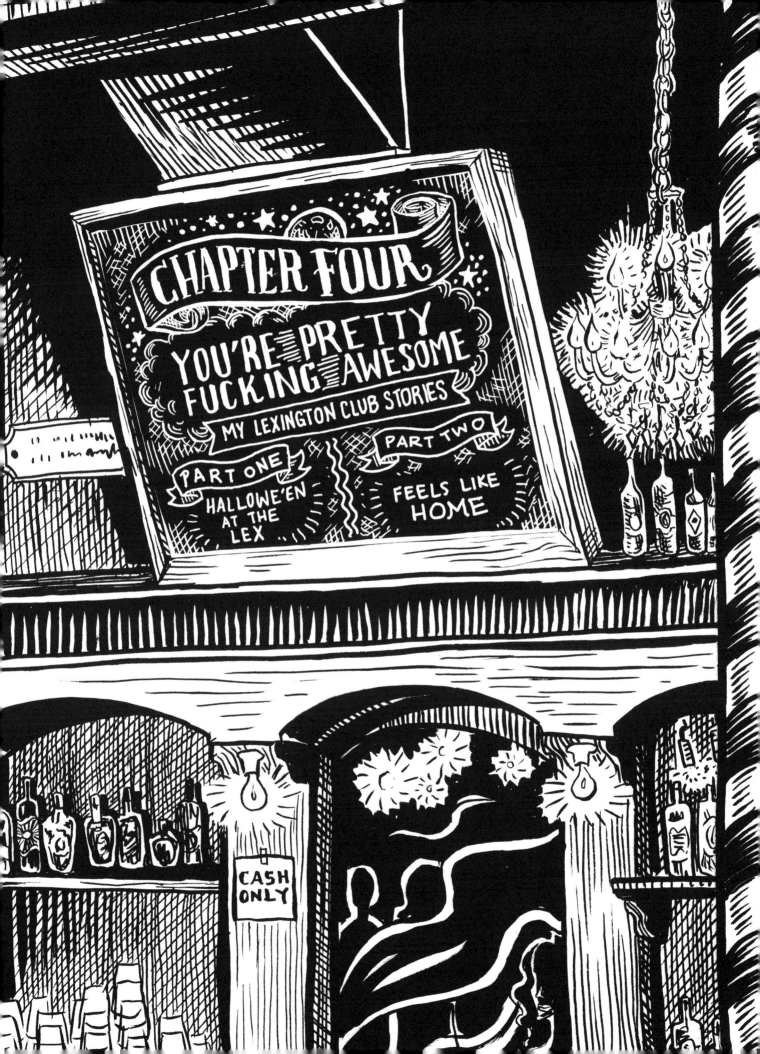

HALLOWEEN AT THE LEX 2014

I CONFESS THAT I WAS PLANNING ON DRAWING AT HOME THIS EVENING, BUT I WAS TOLD:

LAME! IT IS HALLOW-EEN!!

SO, NATURALLY: THE LEX.

I GOT HERE EARLY SO I COULD SET UP AND DRAW. I'M WEARING A SWEATER COVERED IN EYEBALLS...

...AND I HAVE THEM ON MY HANDS, LIKE THE MONSTER FROM PAN'S LABYRINTH. OR LIKE A PERSON WHO SEES A LOT.

THEN, KILL BILL HAPPENED...

AS I DREW THEM, "BLOW" BY BEYONCE CAME ON... YES.

85

"ZE WORKED IN HR AT MY LAST JOB, AND ZE ACTUALLY INTERVIEWED ME..."

tension

AND THEN WHEN WE WERE WORKING TOGETHER, I KEPT DROPPING ALL THESE HINTS THAT I LIKED HIR...

YOU DID?

YES!

THESE TWO WERE NOT IN COSTUME--BUT THEY WERE IN LOVE...

"ANYWAYS, THEN WE WENT TO WATCH MALEFICENT AND THEN TO DRINK SOME GREAT CHAMPAGNE..."

"THEN IT WAS LATE SO SHE JUST INVITED HERSELF OVER, AND I LIVE IN A STUDIO SO THERE WAS NO CHOICE BUT FOR HER TO SLEEP IN MY BED..."

...AND SHE KISSED ME, WHICH WAS SHOCKING BECAUSE I'D BEEN ALWAYS WONDERING IF I SHOULD KISS HER. AND THEN WE ...WERE TOGETHER!

86

I GUESS I SHOULD STOP DRAWING SOON AND SOCIALIZE IN A "NORMAL" WAY, OR I'LL HAVE TO CHANGE THE NAME OF MY SERIES FROM "BISEXUAL TRIALS AND ERRORS" TO "BISEXUAL NOT EVEN TRYING..."

THIS GIRL IS SO HOT. NOW SHE KNOWS... I THINK SO...

SHE HAS A TATTOO THAT SAYS "BREWSKI"

BREWSK

AND I LIKE THE CARPENTER-COWBOY. A LOT. BUT DON'T WANT TO BE TOO FOREWARD.

WHAT are you DRINK-ING??

YOU'RE DOING A SERVICE RIGHT NOW.

NOW THERE ARE BEAUTIFUL, PROFESSIONALLY VERY-SEXY-FEMMES DANCING ON A TABLE... GO FEMMES!!!

AT THIS POINT, THE LIGHTS GO OUT, WHICH SEEMS LIKE A GOOD TIME TO ASK THE BARTENDERS TO HIDE MY BOOK SO I CAN GO ... MINGLE. MAYBE FIND THE COWBOY...

... BUT THE THING THAT NEEDS TO HAPPEN IMMEDIATELY IS THAT I MUST SHOVE THROUGH THE CROWD TO THE BATHROOM. SINCE PEOPLE HAVE BEEN SO KINDLY BUYING ME DRINKS, I MUST NOT BE STOPPED NOW, NO MATTER WHAT.

WHEN I GOT THERE, THE PERSON IN THE STALL WAS TAKING FOREVER. A CUTIE WHO HAD BEEN WATCHING ME BEFORE BANGED THE DOOR ON MY BEHALF.

BAM! BAM! BAM!

THEY ALSO GAVE ME THIS CARD, WITH THEIR EMAIL ON THE BACK.

YOU'RE PRETTY FUCKING AWESOME.
THAT IS ALL.
Keep that shit up.

THEY TOLD ME, WHEN I ASKED WHAT TIME IT WAS...

IT'S LATE -- IF YOU WANT TO BART TO EAST-BAY, YOU PRETTY MUCH HAVE TO GO NOW.

... BUT BEFORE I LEFT, THIS HAPPENED:

IT FELT GREAT, THIS KISS. LIKE I EXPECTED IT WOULD. I WISH IT COULD KEEP GOING...

BUT I HAVE TO LEAVE AND GO HOME, BEFORE I CHANGED INTO A PUMPKIN OR SOMETHING.

THIS WAS A GOOD NIGHT.

UPON READING MY FIRST COMIC, THEY SAID:

YOU LIKE BUTCH GIRLS??

I NEVER WOULD HAVE GUESSED THAT.

BECAUSE YOU'RE KIND OF INBETWEEN YOUR-SELF, TOO*

*BECAUSE SHORT HAIR!

THEN THEY GAVE ME SOME PRO-TIPS...

YOU MIGHT NOT MEET YOUR GIRL AT A BAR. I MET MY EX AT CHURCH.

PRO-TIP ONE:

PROTIP TWO: SOMETIMES IT HELPS TO PRETEND YOU DON'T LIKE THE PERSON YOU DO LIKE.

PROTIP THREE: WHY NOT DATE ANOTHER ARTIST SO YOU CAN JUST... MESH? DO YOU GO TO... CONVENTIONS?

PROTIP FOUR: JUST BE AWARE -- THERE ARE A LOT OF *CRAZY LESBIANS*

YES THE ONES WHO IMMEDIATELY WORSHIP THE GROUND YOU WALK ON... BE CAREFUL.

YES. THOSE ARE THE CRAZY ONES. AND THE ONES WHO SPENT A TON OF TIME DATING MEN.

OH... OK, THANKS.

I FELT LIKE THEY WERE DESCRIBING ME.

SHE GOT A FAKE ID WHEN SHE WAS 16 SO SHE COULD SNEAK INTO LESBIAN BARS, AND CAME TO THE LEX SINCE HER EARLY 20s (NOW IS 38.) SHE SAID THE SENSE OF COMMUNITY AMONG DYKES WAS STRONGER AND MORE FUN WHEN THERE WAS MORE OPPRESSION. I'VE HEARD THIS FROM A FEW PEOPLE.

SHE CONFESSED TO ME:

SOOO THERE'S A GIRL I HOOKED UP WITH MEETING ME HERE AND... I DON'T REMEMBER HER NAME...

SO WHEN HER DATE CAME IN...

HI! I'M ELIZABETH.

I'M LINDA.

WHEN THEY LEFT TOGETHER A FEW DRINKS LATER I WONDERED HOW DIFFERENTLY IT WOULD HAVE GONE.

LINDA SEEMED COOL. I WOULD HAVE REMEMBERED HER NAME.

This woman WALKED IN BRIEFLY -- I DREW HER -- AND NOW I THINK MAYBE SHE'S GONE.

SHE SAID SHE'D NEVER BEEN HERE BEFORE AND WANTED TO SEE IT BEFORE IT CLOSED.

I IMAGINED HER REPORTING BACK TO HER FRIENDS LATER:

LESBIAN BARS ARE **GREAT!** IT SEEMS THAT THE LESBIANS JUST SIT AND DRAW IN BOOKS! WHO KNEW?

photo of draw-ing on phone

I WONDER IF IT BOTHERS THE BAR-TENDERS WHEN SO MANY NEW PEOPLE COME IN -- AFTER THE BAR'S ALREADY BEEN SOLD. EVEN I HAD BEEN HERE ONLY FIVE OR SO TIMES BEFORE I HEARD IT WAS CLOSING.

THIS IS **KATY**, WHO IS AN EXECUTIVE *SUSHI CHEF*-- SHE SAYS SHE JUST DID IT *A LOT* AND REALLY WELL AND DIDN'T LET ANYONE PUSH HER OUT. NOW SHE'S OPENING HER OWN SHOP.

SHE'S BEEN COMING TO THE LEX FOR 5 YEARS.

SHE SAYS PEOPLE DON'T GET HOW MUCH TRAINING AND CRAFT GOES INTO A SINGLE ROLL...

...AND THAT THE LAST PLACE SHE WORKED THEY HIRED AN EXECUTIVE WHO HATED GAY PEOPLE AND TREATED HER SO BADLY THAT SHE HAD TO QUIT...

...BUT IN HER NEW PLACE, SHE'S IN CHARGE AND SHE CAN JUST MAKE EXCELLENT FUCKING FOOD.

96

MY FRIENDS DECLAN, JAI AND DARCY SHOWED UP AND ENCOURAGED ME TO

STOP DRAWING AND DANCE WITH US!

I WAS INTO THE WOMAN I WAS DRAWING AT THE MOMENT, SO I SAID:

DO YOU WANT TO DANCE?

YES.

AS IF BY THE GRACE OF GOD, "LIKE A PRAYER" CAME ON THE JUKEBOX AS SOON AS WE STOOD UP. WE SANG EVERY WORD.

♪LIFE IS A MYSTERY.. EVERYONE MUST STAND ALONE..

♪I HEAR YOU CALL MY NAME.. AND IT FEELS LIKE HOME.

THAT WAS FUN. I REMEMBER DANCING TO THAT SONG IN HIGH SCHOOL WHEN IT CAME OUT.

...I THINK I WAS IN THE WOMB WHEN THAT SONG CAME OUT.

SORRY -- I DIDN'T REALIZE I COULD HAVE BEEN YOUR MOTHER...

... IF I HAD BEEN, YOU KNOW, A FAST TEEN.

MY FRIENDS INQUIRED:

HEY -- WHERE'S YOUR NEW FRIEND?

SHE THINKS WE'RE GENERATIONALLY INAPPROPRIATE.

♪ driver roll up the PARTITION PLEASE ♪

OH, PSHAW. SHE'S HOT! GO TALK TO HER SOME MORE!

I USUALLY DATE OLDER WOMEN. AND YOU'RE AN OLD SOUL...

BUT THE LAST GIRL I WAS SEEING WAS YOUNG--

--I HAVE TO GO. BUT, YOU SHOULD GO FOR IT.

DARCY'S LEAVING? WHAT HAPPENED?

I'M NOT SURE...

FOR THE REST OF THE EVENING DECLAN, JAI AND I DANCED WITH THREE WOMEN WE'D MET. ONE OF THEM WAS IN THE ARMY AND BEING DEPLOYED ON WEDNESDAY.

...TO NEPAL. THE ARMY IS BORING-- THIS IS EXCITING!

WE FOUND LOVE IN A HOPELESS PLACE

AS WE DANCED TO RIHANNA AND TINA TURNER FROM THE JUKEBOX, I NOTICED HOW NICE IT WAS TO BE OUT AT NIGHT WITHOUT WORRYING ABOUT THE THREAT-- OR ACTUALITY-- OF CREEPY, AGGRESSIVE MEN.

♫♫ WHAT'S LOVE GOT TO DO WITH IT? ♫

UNLIKE MANY OF THE REGULARS AT THE LEX, MY QUEERNESS HAD NEVER BROUGHT ME ANY HARDSHIP OR PREJUDICE. BUT BEING FEMALE HAS AT TIMES BEEN A STRUGGLE, AND SOMETIMES BEEN REALLY SCARY. WHICH MAY BE WHY THIS PREDOMINANTLY FEMALE BAR FEELS SO SAFE AND FUN.

I DANCED AWKWARDLY...

DREW REALLY WELL...

IS DANCING FOR DRAWING

...AND LEFT WITH JAI AND DECLAN FOR EAST BAY, ALL OF US IN HIGH SPIRITS.

yaaay weekend!

GOODNIGHT LEX

GOODNIGHT QUEERS

AND GOODNIGHT BEERS,

GOODNIGHT JUKEBOX FOR OUR EARS...

GOODNIGHT SAN FRANCISCO RULES,

PLEASE NO E-CIGS NO GOOGLE GLASS

GOODNIGHT WOMEN PLAYING POOL.

GOODNIGHT LOCAL ART ON THE WALLS...

BAGGAGE

GOODNIGHT DRAWINGS ALL OVER THE STALLS.

GOODNIGHT BUTCHES, GOODNIGHT FEMMES,

GOODNIGHT FOLKS JUST BEING THEM.

HA HA HA HA HA

GOODNIGHT COCKTAILS, STRONG & CHEAP

BLUEBERRY SMASH ♥

GOODNIGHT ARCADE MACHINES THAT BLINK.

GOODNIGHT ICONIC BAR for DYKES— we're SAD YOU HAVE TO TURN OFF THE LIGHTS.

*BY 'THERPS' WE MEAN 'MY THERAPIST.' FOR MORE, CHECK OUT THE REAL TINA'S BLOG, LESSONSFROMTHERPS.COM

WHAT ABOUT THIS KITTEN, POSIE? SHE'S A LITTLE SHY...

SHE'S VERY CUTE, BUT... HMM.

OR IF YOU'D CONSIDER A CAT THAT'S NOT A NEWBORN, THERE'S CHARLIE HERE...

OH HI, BUDDY!

DO YOU WANNA COME STAY WITH ME AND BE MY CAT?

I THINK HE'S THE ONE.

YESH...

OKAY! DO YOU HAVE EVERYTHING YOU NEED TO TAKE CARE OF A YEAR-OLD KITTEN!

LET'S PUT HIM DOWN FOR A LITTLE BIT AND GRAB SOME PIZZA AROUND THE CORNER.

BUT...

I KNOW, IT'S SAD. BUT IT'S LIKE NINE THIRTY AND I'M STARVING.

SO, CAN I STAY OVERNIGHT?... AND POSSIBLY FOREVER?

...ACTUALLY, I WAS THINKING IT MIGHT BE BEST IF YOU WENT HOME AFTER PIZZA SO HOPKINS KNOWS I'M HIS HUMAN-MAMA.

BUT YOU SHOULD VISIT ALL THE TIME, OOOBVS.

YEAH NO, THAT MAKES SENSE.

I KNOW, IT'S A BUMMER. ARE YOU OKAY?

BECCA THE CAT LADY TOTALLY THOUGHT WE WERE A LESBIAN COUPLE.

...YEAH, PROBABLY...

...SORRY, I JUST...

OKAY, WHY DON'T YOU TAKE A FEW MINUTES TO SAY BYE FOR TONIGHT.

HI, HOPS.

SORRY, I CAN'T SEEM TO STOP. I HAVEN'T CRIED IN ALMOST TWO YEARS...

...SINCE JAMES AND I BROKE UP. WE HAD THIS CRAZY PLAN THAT HE WAS GOING TO COME SEE ME IN A MONTH NOW THAT I DON'T LIVE WITH MY PARENTS AND MY HOUSEMATES ARE GONNA BE AWAY...

...HE HAD A PLANE TICKET AND EVERYTHING BUT THERPS SAID IT WAS A TERRIBLE PLAN. I JUST... REALLY MISS HIM.

Meow Mi

I EVEN HAVE MY OWN PIANO NOW. I'VE BEEN PRACTICING. ...OH WELL...

I'VE GOTTA GO NOW. KEEP TINA COMPANY 'TIL I GET BACK, OKAY?

I'M GLAD SHE PICKED YOU. ♡

MY HOUSEMATES ARE AWAY FOR THE HOLIDAY AND JAMES CANCELED HIS FLIGHT, SO I HAVE MY NEW PLACE TO MYSELF.

SO. I'VE BEEN IN BED...

...WATCHING THE VAMPIRE DIARIES FOR SIX STRAIGHT DAYS.

JAMES LOVES THE FROZEN WHITE-CHRISTMAS THING SO HE'S PROBABLY HAPPIER OUT EAST.

I NEVER GOT WHY HE PREFERS THE COLD...

KNOCK
KNOCK

HE SAID HE LOVED GETTING WARM WITH ME UNDER THE COVERS AND DRINKING HOT CHOCOLATE...

KNOCK

...WATCHING THE SNOW DRIFT OUTSIDE AND PILE UP ON THE WINDOW AND BRANCHES

Door Dash.

...AND SNUGGLING FOR SHARED BODY HEAT THROUGH THE FRIGID LONG NIGHTS.

Thank you.

I GUESS THAT HAD BEEN NICE.

I MISS HOW HE USED TO WARM UP MY HANDS WITH HIS HANDS.

BZZZ..
BZZZ...

SAMSUNG
4:22
You have a new match on Tinder
You have a new message on Tinder
12/24/15

122

I'LL WEAR MY RED SWEATER AND BLACK SKIRT. AND LIPSTICK.

I NEED A HAIRCUT BEFORE WORK STARTS UP AGAIN.

SOMETIMES I MISS HAVING LONG HAIR, AND BEING THIN. BEING "PRETTY."

JAMES SENT THAT "YOU ARE ABOUT TO GET SO MUCH PUSSY" EMAIL WHEN I CUT IT...

BUT IN 2013 WHEN I SLIMMED DOWN AND GREW OUT MY HAIR HE TOLD ME HOW SMALL AND BREAKABLE I FELT WHILE HE FUCKED ME.

HE SAID IT BY ACCIDENT AT FIRST...

BUT THEN I ASKED HIM TO KEEP SAYING IT.

WOULD HE EVEN STILL BE ATTRACTED TO ME IF HE HAD VISITED?

I GOT DISTRACTED BY THE LASAGNA.

THANK YOU FOR COOKING! IT SAYS ON YOUR PROFILE YOU WORK AT A BAKERY?

HA! FOR NOW. IT'S MOSTLY FROSTING CAKES AND DECORATING HOLIDAY COOKIES THESE DAYS...

WELL, CAKE IS GREAT. AND YOU LIKE TO SING?

COOL.

YEAH, WHEN I LIVED IN OREGON I PERFORMED IN A CHOIR. I'M TRAINED CLASSICALLY, ALTO. BUT I HAVEN'T FOUND PEOPLE OUT HERE TO SING WITH YET.

ANYWAYS, THIS IS FOR YOU...

THANKS! YOU MADE ME LOOK SO PRETTY!

OH PLEASE.

125

HAVE YOU LIVED AROUND HERE FOR A LONG TIME?

IN CALIFORNIA FOR THREE YEARS BUT I JUST MOVED TO OAKLAND SIX MONTHS AGO.

OH, COOL. I ACTUALLY JUST MOVED TO THE BAY A WEEK AGO.

HOW ARE YOU LIKING IT SO FAR?

IT'S... A BIG CHANGE. I MOVED SUDDENLY AND I HAVE A LOT OF HOUSEMATES.

SOME OF THEM ARE IN TOWN SO I FIGURED WE COULD JUST EAT IN MY BEDROOM.

OKAY.

THIS IS IT!... ARE YOU ALLERGIC TO ANY ANIMALS?

NO...

OKAY GOOD...

OOOH!

THAT WAS REALLY PRETTY... THANK YOU! SORRY, WHERE'S YOUR BATHROOM?

HAHA, THANKS. THE BATHROOM'S TO THE RIGHT, SKIP TWO BEDROOMS AND YOU'LL SEE IT.

IT'S OKAY... EVERYTHING IS FINE...

EVERYTHING IS FINE...

JESUS FUCKING CHRIST.

THIS MERLOT IS NICE. THANKS FOR BRINGING IT.

YEAH, I THINK I'LL HAVE ANOTHER GLASS.

WANNA COME LIE DOWN? WE CAN WATCH NETFLIX AND WORK LET ME KEEP THE PASTRIES WE DIDN'T SELL TODAY.

A FEW WEEKS AGO MY (NOW EX) BOYFRIEND AND I WERE ON A ROADTRIP FROM PORTLAND TO MEXICO FOR OUR VACATION. OR SO I *THOUGHT.* ANYWAYS HIS PARENTS LIVE IN BERKELEY AND WE STOPPED TO SEE THEM FOR A NIGHT, AND HE *BROKE UP* WITH ME BECAUSE HE WAS SECRETLY OUT OF MONEY AND HAD TO STAY THERE...

...OH AND OF COURSE IT WAS *HIS* CAR.

WAIT... *WHAT?!* OH MY GOD...

YEAH. BUT I'VE ALWAYS WANTED TO LIVE OUT HERE, AND A ROOM IN THIS HOUSE WAS OPEN SO I'M MAKING IT WORK.

IT JUST SOUNDS *SUDDEN.*

OH, IT WAS. BUT SOMETIMES SUDDEN SHOCKS CAN LEAD TO BETTER TIMES.

HE WASN'T ALL THAT GREAT.

HAH! WELL, THIS IS MY RIDE...

... IT WAS NICE TO MEET YOU, DRU! THANKS FOR DINNER!

OH WELL.

AM I *REALLY* THAT UNTOUCHABLE?

I MEAN... MAYBE.

I GUESS IT'S NOT A HUGE SHOCK THAT *THEY* DIDN'T *SEE ME* IN THAT WAY.

I GUESS THEY WERE LONELY.

IS THIS YOUR HOUSE, MISS?

OH YES, WAIT A SEC...

MERRY CHRISTMAS, THANKS FOR DRIVING ME TONIGHT.

THANKS MISS.

CHAPTER SEVEN
LUCKY TO BE

JANUARY 1st, 2016

THIS WILL BE THE YEAR WHEN I GET THIS **WEIGHT** BACK OFF. ONCE I'M THIN AGAIN IT'LL BE *SO MUCH* EASIER TO *DATE* AND *FIND* *LOVE!*

ME, 2013

JANUARY 6TH, 2016

FUCK IT, I WANT A SUPER BURRITO.

WALKING TO OLE OLE

HEY!!

MAYBE I CAN SAVE HALF OF IT FOR LATER...

YOU *STOLE* MY *BABY!*

I FOUND THE LENS AND PICKED IT UP, GOING AS SLOWLY AS POSSIBLE TO AVOID PASSING OUT.

GRIFFIN FROM WORK DROVE ME TO THE HOSPITAL.

AND *THEN* I CAN HAVE SUPER BURRITO?

SURE, ONCE YOU GET CHECKED OUT...

GIDDY WITH SHOCK

after my scans

YOU SUFFERED A MINOR CONCUSSION. I'M RECOMMENDING YOU TAKE TIME OFF WORK FOR BRAIN REST.

OKAY, I CAN STAY HOME...

ME & NETFLIX HIT THE *SHEETS!*

← GRIFFIN BROUGHT MY BURRITO # HERO.

...WHAT I MEAN IS, YOU SHOULD *TOTALLY* REST YOUR BRAIN, SO IT HEALS. SO NO TV OR RADIO, NO READING, NO FACEBOOK, NO MENTAL EXERTION WHATSOEVER.

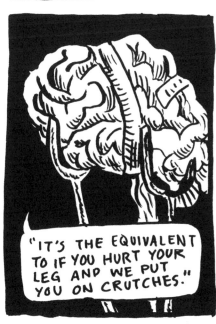

"IT'S THE EQUIVALENT TO IF YOU HURT YOUR LEG AND WE PUT YOU ON CRUTCHES."

SO...I CAN'T LISTEN TO THE PODCAST VERSION OF THE *RACHEL MADDOW SHOW* AT 8PM ON WEEKDAYS?

I'M AFRAID NOT UNTIL YOU'RE ALL BETTER.

AS MY BRAIN HEALED, I AMENDED MY NEW YEAR'S RESOLUTION. RATHER THAN COMMITTING TO SHRINK MYSELF, I'D JUST LEARN TO LOVE MY BODY NOW.

WHEN I FELL BACK INTO OLD HABITS...

UGGH MY LIFE WOULD BE SO MUCH BETTER IF I WAS THIN AND HOT LIKE *THAT* GIRL.

...I CONSIDERED MY OWN BODY MORE TENDERLY, AND LET GO OF THE CRITICAL VOICE...

...AND MY RESTING-BRAIN HARMONY ROSE BACK UP.

BY FEBRUARY, I PUT ON MY SIZE SIXTEEN JEANS WITHOUT SCOLDING MYSELF FOR BEING "GROSS..."

...AND A WEEK LATER, I DIDN'T *THINK* ABOUT MY PANT SIZE...

...I THOUGHT ABOUT APPLYING FOR A NEW JOB OR MAKING NEW COMICS.

I DIDN'T HAVE TO GO THROUGH A YEAR OF PENANCE, DIET AND DEPRIVATION TO LOVE MY BODY MORE THAN I EVER HAD...

I JUST TREATED MYSELF WITH *KINDNESS*.

ON MARCH 2ND, 2016, I WON A *MOTH* STORY SLAM WITH THE THEME "*WITNESS.*" I SPOKE ABOUT GETTING PUNCHED IN THE FACE AND NOONE WANTING TO HELP FIND MY MISSING LENS.

I WAS GOING UP TO THESE *BUSINESS MEN* TO SAY "EXCUSE ME... I WAS JUST HIT IN THE HEAD. MY GLASSES ARE BROKEN. CAN YOU HELP ME PLEASE? (SHAKES NO)

I THINK THEY *THOUGHT* I WAS SAYING: EXCUSE ME, DO YOU HAVE A MINUTE FOR THE ENVIRONMENT?

WINNING MEANT I'D GET TO PERFORM AT THE *CASTRO THEATRE* FOR THE GRAND SLAM.

I WAS *SO EXCITED* TO BE RECOGNIZED FOR ART THAT WASN'T DRAWING! IT WAS JUST ME AND MY STORY THEY LOVED.

ON STAGE, NOBODY CARED THAT I WAS FAT.

NO ONE IN THE AUDIENCE RECOILED OR THREW UP OVER THE FACT THAT I LOVED SUPER BURRITOS.

CHAPTER EIGHT
SMOOTHER

MAR 10TH, 2016 - TINA'S APARTMENT

EEEEEE SHE TEXTED

OOH! THE GIRL FROM THE SHOW?

THE PREVIOUS NIGHT I'D PERFORMED AT DIXIE DE LA TOUR'S *BAWDY STORYTELLING.*

...SO I DREW THE HOTTEST WOMAN IN THE ROOM. IF *SHE* LIKED ME, THEN NO ONE ELSE WOULD BE INTIMIDATING ANYMORE.

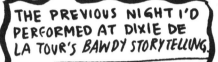

IT'S LIKE THE MOTH BUT FOR TRUE *SEXY* STORIES.*

BEFORE I GOT UP TO TELL MY EROTIC STORY WAS ~~NERVOUS~~ SCARED SHITLESS...

*IT'S AN EXCELLENT PRODUCTION - EVERYONE SHOULD GO!

here it is you.

OH, THANKS...

I'M CASEY.

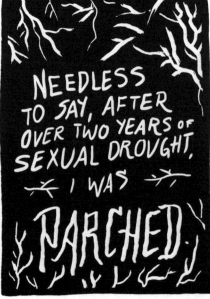

ONCE I WAS UP ON STAGE, I WASN'T NERVOUS--I LOVE PERFORMING AND I FELT GLAMOROUS AND POWERFUL. CASEY ASKED FOR MY NUMBER AFTERWARDS...

AND NOW...

So, thanks :) 5:43

How's your day? 5:43

I'm doing well. How are you? I'm glad you texted. 6:20

It's been a long damn day and I'm exhausted. Gonna make myself a cocktail and wind on down. 6:20

You certainly made an impression

LOOK!!

O-M-GEE, YOU ARE FINALLY GONNA GET LAID.

NEEDLESS TO SAY, AFTER OVER TWO YEARS OF SEXUAL DROUGHT, I WAS

PARCHED.

WE MET UP AT DOGWOOD, A BAR IN OAKLAND. I WORE MY BEST MAKEUP.

THIS IS A COOL PLACE. I JUST MOVED TO CALIFORNIA A FEW WEEKS AGO FOR WORK.

I HAVEN'T ACTUALLY BEEN HERE EITHER EVEN THOUGH I LIVE SUPER CLOSE BY. WHERE ARE YOU FROM?

DALLAS MOST RECENTLY, BUT BEFORE THAT I LIVED IN NEW ORLEANS AND THAT FELT WAY MORE LIKE HOME. I ONCE RAN A READING SERIES THERE.

OH, COOL! SO WHAT'S THE NEW JOB?

I WORK AT DICTIONARY DOT COM.

Mar 11th

pretty green shirt & black skirt

WELL, THIS EVAPORATED. WOULD YOU LIKE ANOTHER GIN + TONIC?

YES PLEASE, THANK YOU.

SHE MOVED THROUGH THE BAR LIKE IT WAS HER HOMETOWN FAVORITE.

SO... CAN I DRAW YOU AGAIN, BUT LIKE, A NICER ONE?

SURE!

I REALLY LIKED HER HAIR AND DIMPLES.

HER SKIN LOOKED VERY SOFT

SHE SAID SHE'S HAD THIS BADASS LEATHER JACKET SINCE SHE WAS THIRTEEN

WE TALKED ABOUT COMICS AND STORYTELLING AND THE ENGLISH LANGUAGE AND ART.

SHE DIDN'T HAVE A SOUTHERN DRAWL BUT HER VOICE DEFINITELY PACKED EXTRA CHARM & SWAGGER

I LOVED HOW SHE SPOKE EMPHATICALLY... WITH HER VOICE AND HANDS

THE DRINKS KICKED IN & I IMAGINED HER HANDS ON ME.

I LIKED HER BLUE PLAID SHIRT.

HERE YOU GO. AS YOU CAN TELL, DRAWING IS KIND OF MY LINE.

HONESTLY-- FOR ME, I REALLY LIKED THAT DRAWING, AND THIS ONE. BUT I ASKED FOR YOUR NUMBER BECAUSE OF YOUR STORY...

... HOW YOU HELD THAT AUDIENCE IN THE PALM OF YOUR HAND

MM. YEP, I LIKE THAT BETTER THAN TEQUILA.

RIGHT? IT'S SMOOTHER.

I HAVE TO TELL YOU SOMETHING...

OKAY.

IT'S KIND OF AWKWARD.

I'VE NEVER... UH... BEEN WITH A WOMAN BEFORE. I MEAN, I'VE ALWAYS BEEN *INTO* WOMEN...

AND *FOR SURE* I LIKE KISSING WOMEN.

IT'S THE BEST.

I'VE JUST NEVER GONE *BEYOND* KISSING. AND I WANT TO! A LOT. JUST THOUGHT YOU SHOULD KNOW... IN CASE...

I MEAN I KNOW FOR SOME PEOPLE THAT CHANGES THINGS SO I WANTED TO BE UPFRONT.

BUT. I LIKE YOU. SO... YEAH.

I'M DONE NOW.

WELL. I APPRECIATE YOU TELLING ME. AND IT'S ALRIGHT...

I HAVE ENOUGH EXPERIENCE FOR THE BOTH OF US.

160

LET'S GET OUT OF HERE.

MHM. LET'S.

SO... YOU LIVE IN HAYWARD?

YEAH. IT'S KINDA FAR.

I LIVE REALLY CLOSE TO HERE, ACTUALLY. BUT MY ROOM IS A HUGE MESS.*

* WHYYYY...

OH I WOULDN'T MIND. LITERALLY ALL I HAVE IN CALIFORNIA SO FAR IS A BED AND ONE SUITCASE OF MY THINGS.

BUT, I THINK LET'S EACH GO HOME TONIGHT, AND TEXT TOMORROW.

OH.. OKAY.

SO LET'S EACH CALL AN UBER...

CASEY'S PROFILE KIND OF LOOKED LIKE THE MOON IN THE LAMPLIGHT...

...AND WHEN SHE WRAPPED HER ARM AROUND ME...

... I FELT IT DOWN TO MY TOES.

163

SIIIIGHH...

WHEN SHE HAD PULLED AWAY SHE SMILED — WAS SHE LAUGHING AT HOW EAGER I WAS?

ISN'T THAT YOUR RIDE?

MY LIPS WERE STILL BURNING. I HOPED MY DRIVER COULDN'T TELL HOW TURNED ON I WAS.

me: You teeassse. I'm home. My room is about to get SO CLEAN.

My room is about to get SO CLEAN.

Don't say I didn't warn you.

Promise it'll be worth it.

SO. SHE WAS COCKY...

AND THAT MADE HER EVEN HOTTER.

SHE INVITED ME TO HER APARTMENT THE NEXT EVENING. IT WAS GONNA HAPPEN!!

SORRY FOR THE PAUSE, PASSENGERS, WE HAVE A BIT OF A TRAFFIC JAM AT THE LAKE MERRIT STOP AND THEN WE'LL GET YOU MOVING AGAIN WHEN WE GET THE ALL-CLEAR.

WHAT IF AFTER ALL THIS TIME I DIDN'T ACTUALLY *LIKE* SEX WITH WOMEN?

OR NOT AS MUCH?

OR WHAT IF I *LOVED* IT BUT WAS *BAD* AT IT?

BUT EVER SINCE LAST NIGHT MY BODY FELT FLUSH WITH DESIRE.

AND I FELT <u>SEXY</u>.

THE KISS WOULDN'T HAVE BEEN *THAT* LONG AND EXPLOSIVE IF THERE WASN'T *CHEMISTRY*.

RIGHT..?

KNOCK KNOCK

HEY. COME IN.

167

BEFORE I'D ONLY EVER HAD SEX WITH JAMES. AND IT WAS GREAT...

FUUUCKK..

BUT LIKE THE WOMAN AT THE LEX PREDICTED, THIS WAS NEW AND DIFFERENT AND EUPHORIC IN WAYS...

...THAT I HADN'T IMAGINED BEFORE IT HAPPENED.

I KEPT SEEING CASEY AND THE SEX GOT EVEN BETTER...

...AS SHE SHOWED ME HOW TO RECIPROCATE THE PLEASURE SHE GAVE ME...

...AND AS I LEARNED MORE ABOUT HER AS A PERSON. NEITHER OF US HAD EVER BEEN TO SANTA CRUZ, SO ONE DAY SHE DROVE US DOWN.

I'M SO GLAD TO FINALLY LIVE IN A PLACE WHERE I CAN SEE THE OCEAN WHENEVER I WANT. IT MAKES ME FEEL FREE... SMALL IN A GOOD WAY.

THERE ARE THESE WEIRD HUMAN-MADE LAKES IN DALLAS THAT MADE ME FEEL EVEN MORE LANDLOCKED AND STUCK THERE...

...BUT I'M HERE NOW.

I WAS ALSO LEARNING A TON ABOUT WHO *I* WAS AS A PERSON.

LIKE -- I USED TO THINK I DIDN'T ENJOY RECEIVING ORAL SEX.

FALSE. ORAL IS THE *BEST!...*

((... OKAY, MAYBE BESIDES FISTING.))

HOW DID YOU EVEN...

I REALIZED I AM HARD-WIRED TO BE *KINKY* AND *SUBBY...*

...AND THAT I SHOULD *ENJOY* AND *RELISH* THAT PART OF MYSELF.

I FINALLY BELIEVED THAT MY BODY WAS *BEAUTIFUL & SEXY*

AS IT IS...

... AND THAT THINNESS & TRADITIONAL BEAUTY

JUNE 2016

I LOVE YOU.

ARE NOT PREREQUISITES FOR FINDING LOVE.

I LEARNED THAT THERE HAD BEEN *NOTHING WRONG* WITH ME ON THE DATES THAT DIDN'T GO AS I HAD HOPED...

I JUST REALLY WANT TO BE YOUR FRIEND.*

*STILL FRIENDS BTW!

... I'D JUST NEEDED TO PUT MYSELF *OUT* THERE, OVER AND OVER AGAIN, SAME AS EVERYONE.

I ALSO REALIZED THAT EVEN THOUGH DRAWING PEOPLE IS SOMETHING I *LOVE* AND EXCEL AT, IT'S NOT SOMETHING I *HAVE* TO DO TO BE LIKED.

MAYBE APPROACHING ATTRACTIVE WOMEN WITH DRAWINGS AND *"PLEASE LOVE ME"* WRITTEN ON MY FACE ACTUALLY SIGNALLED INSECURITY.

you are preeeetty.

Thanks!

I CARRY MYSELF DIFFERENTLY NOW. I FEEL MORE SECURE IN MY QUEERNESS... BUT ALSO MORE SECURE IN MY OWN WORTH,

WHETHER I'M CURRENTLY DATING OR NOT,

WHETHER I ONE DAY LOSE WEIGHT OR NOT,

WHETHER I'M BURIED IN MY SKETCH-BOOK OR NOT.

THE MOTH

MOTH GRAND SLAM, CASTRO THEATRE, OCT 2016.

ON STAGE WITH JUST *ME* AND A *MIC*, I CAN MOVE PEOPLE TO LAUGHTER OR TEARS, JUST BY TELLING THEM STORIES.

IN BED BY MYSELF AT THE END OF THE DAY, I CAN GO TO SLEEP WITHOUT WANTING TO FIX MYSELF.

APPENDIX I
OFF THE CHARTS

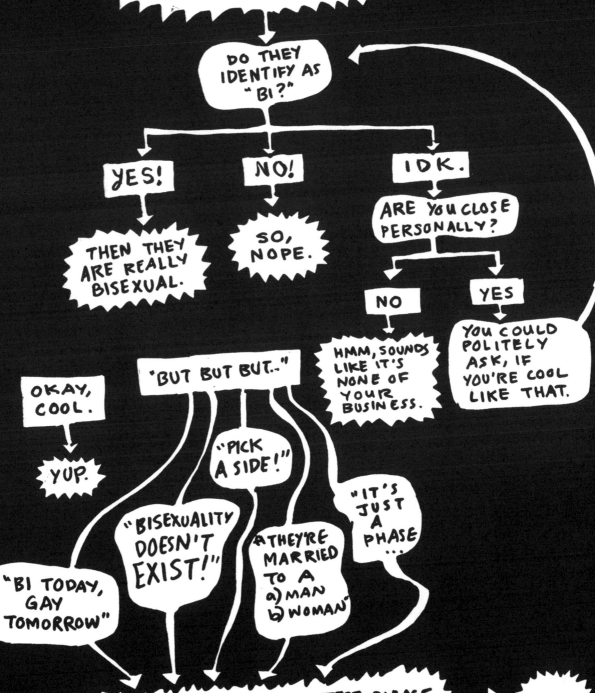

HOW to DE-ESCALATE YOUR OBSESSIVE CRUSH

IN JUST TWELVE ~~EASY~~ STEPS!!

ARE YOU TIRED OF YOUR LIFE BEING LIKE **THIS**?

crush crush crush crush crush crush crush

1 LIKE A RECOVERING ALCOHOLIC, THE FIRST STEP TO DE-ESCALATING YOUR CRUSH IS TO ADMIT THAT IT HAS TAKEN OVER YOUR LIFE...

CRUSH CRUSH CRUSH CRUSH CRUSH CRUSH CRUSH CRUSH CRUSH CRUSH CRUSH CRUSH CRUSH

2 AND YOU HAVE TO DECIDE YOU <u>REALLY</u> WANT TO STOP. WHICH FRANKLY-- YOU PROBABLY DON'T. BUT IF YOU ARE <u>COMMITTED</u>, TRY THE REST:

CRUSH CRUSH CR-- OTHER THINGS?!

3 IF IT'S POSSIBLE --YOU SHOULD CONFESS YOUR FEELINGS DIRECTLY.

UM, SO I KINDA WANT TO MAKE OUT WITH YOU...

THIS MAY SEEM LIKE THE OPPOSITE OF LETTING GO, BUT WHAT WILL PROBABLY HAPPEN IS THIS:

I DON'T KNOW, DUDE...I JUST WANT TO BE YOUR FRIEND.

WHICH IS HELPFULL...

...SO YOU CAN JUST MOVE ON WITH YOUR SHIT WITH FEWER WHAT-IFS.

~~CRUSH~~ ~~CRUSH~~ ~~CRUSH~~ ~~CRUSH~~ ~~CRUSH~~ ~~CRUSH~~

AFTER LISTENING TO "HEART LIKE A WHEEL" ON LOOP 1,000 TIMES.

184

4 WHETHER OR NOT YOU DID STEP THREE, YOU SHOULD STOP TALKING ABOUT YOUR CRUSH TO YOUR FRIENDS.

how's it going?

Cr-r-r-azy day at work!

THEY WILL **NOT** MIND.

5 SPEAKING OF YOUR FRIENDS, YOU PROBABLY OWE THEM EACH A DRINK...

what's up in YOUR life?

CLINK

...AND YOU SHOULD ASK HOW **THEY** ARE DOING.

6 RESTRICT CONTACT WITH YOUR CRUSH.

crush: want to drop all your plans and come see me right now?

you: no-- i have PLANS.

NOT NECESSARILY 100%- BUT, DEFINITELY STOP SPENDING TIME PLOTTING HOW TO SEE THEM AND WHAT TO SAY.

7 INDULGE IN OTHER MINI-CRUSHES...

BUT- TAKE IT EASY! DON'T RE-OBSESS!

8 WITH YOUR NEW FREE BRAIN CAPACITY, PERSUE A HOBBY.

DO YOU DRAW? COOK? PLAY MUSIC OR SPORTS? IF NOT... *LEARN.*

9 MAKE A LIST ON YOUR PHONE OF LITERALLY **ANYTHING** YOU LIKE BESIDES YOUR CRUSH.

TREES
COMICS
PORTRAITS
DRAWING
FRIENDS
COLORS
HARRY POTTER

WHEN YOUR BRAIN GOES TO CRUSHTOWN ON AUTO-PILOT, REFER TO YOUR LIST.

10 STOP STALKING THEIR SOCIAL MEDIA PROFILES.

trouble.

STEP **AWAY** FROM THE FACEBOOK PHOTO ALBUMS.

11 WORK OUT. LIFT WEIGHTS. RUN AROUND.

(photo not found)

FOR HAPPY BRAIN CHEMICALS AND INCREASED CONFIDENCE.

12. STRIVE FOR PROGRESS, NOT PERFECTION.

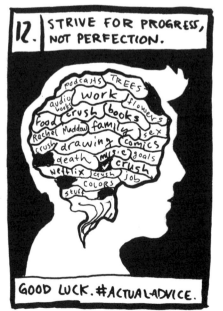

podcasts TREES
audio books work flowers
food crush books
Rachel Maddow family sex
crush drawing comics
death music goals
Netflix crush job
colors
stuff ✓crush

GOOD LUCK. #ACTUALADVICE.

191

NOELLE

ME: WHAT'S YOUR FAVORITE MEMORY OF THIS PLACE?

NOELLE: IT'S A BAR! I DON'T REMEMBER MUCH WHEN I LEAVE HERE.
I USED TO STAY HERE UNTIL 6AM WITH THE OLD MANAGER-- I'D CLEAN AND SHE'D SMOKE. WE WEREN'T EVEN ON DRUGS--JUST TALKING.

I GOT THIS JACKET TODAY. AT THE MACY'S KIDS' DEPARTMENT.

I'VE BEEN IN THIS CITY COMING HERE FOR 12 YEARS, AND I WORKED HERE AS A BOUNCER FOR FOUR. SO IT REALLY IS MY HOME NOW.

IF THEY PUT FUCKING CONDOS HERE I SAY WE SHOW UP AND GET DRUNK IN PEOPLE'S LIVING ROOMS. BUT IF IT'S A BULLSHIT BAR I WON'T SUPPORT IT.

CHLOE KILLS ME. I WANTED TO DRINK THROUGHOUT THE NIGHT-- AND NOW, FUCK, THIS IS A CUP OF VODKA.

I'M A NEW YORKER. I DON'T HAVE FAKE OPINIONS.

I FEEL LIKE TO DRAW ME YOU SHOULD JUST MAKE A WHIRLWIND AND SAY: "THIS IS NOELLE SKOOL, SHE WOULDN'T STAY STILL!"

I WANT TO KEEP OUR COMMUNITY TOGETHER-- AT A BAR THAT'S DIVEY, EVEN UNDERGROUND, FOR THE FUCKING QUEER-ALTERNATIVE KIDS -- THE WEIRDOS. THAT WAS HERE.

I TURNED TWENTY ONE HERE..

I'VE NEVER BEEN SO DRUNK...BUT I PACED MYSELF, SO IT WASN'T AS GNARLY AS IT COULD HAVE BEEN ...

"ONE TIME OUTSIDE OF THIS BAR, A MAN WALKED UP TO A TRANS WOMAN AND SAID-- 'HEY MAN, HAVE A CIGARETTE??

excuse me?

AND SHE PUNCHED HIM IN THE FACE AND GAVE HIM A BLOODY NOSE!

AND THEN WE WERE LIKE-- DUDE, THAT WAS YOUR BAD. "

WTF??

PRONOUNS, YO.

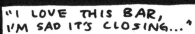

THE LEXINGTON CLUB CLOSED IN APRIL
2015. FOR MORE MEMORIES AND
PORTRAITS, PLEASE SEE MY 80-PAGE
LEXINGTON CLUB BOOK AT
WWW.ELIZABETHDREWYOU.COM.

RESOURCES AND RECOMMENDATIONS

If you're in trouble and need support, you're not alone.

RAINN hotline
For matters relating to rape, sexual assault, and incest.
1-800-656-4673 | rainn.org

Suicide Prevention Lifeline
1-800-273-8255

The Trevor Project Hotline
For LGBT+ people at risk of suicide. **1-866-488-7386**

The National Domestic Violence Hotline
1-800-787-3224

BOOK RECOMMENDATIONS

Shrill: Notes from a Loud Woman by Lindy West
After the events of the story in this comic, I read *Shrill: Notes from a Loud Woman* by Lindy West. Although I was already on the way there, reading this book gave me more language and courage to resist fat-shaming and love myself. If the body positive parts of *Bisexual Trials and Errors* resonate with you, I especially recommend this book.

The Ultimate Guide to Kink: BDSM, Role Play and the Erotic Edge
In my comics, I reference both happy kinky sex, and a time when the kink I was involved with was unhealthy and dangerous. This book, edited by Tristan Taormino, emphasizes the "safe, sane, and consensual", gives some practical tips, and is a great primer for people who want to safely explore edgier sex.

Understanding Comics by Scott McCloud
McCloud's book gives a lot of history, theory, and analysis of comics in an engaging comic format.

Drawing Words and Writing Pictures by Jessica Abel and Matt Madden.
This book includes discrete lessons, with homework, on issues such as inking and story arc.

QUEER COMICS RESOURCES

Kickstarter
An amazing place to find up and coming queer projects. Just go to **kickstarter.com** and search away!

MariNaomi's databases
A great place to find new queer cartoonists and cartoonists of color, searchable by pronoun, name and ethnicity.
queercartoonists.com | cartoonistsofcolor.com

Prism Comics

A 501(c)3 non-profit organization that promotes awareness of lesbian, gay, bisexual, and transgender creators, stories, characters, and readers in the comics industry. **prismcomics.org**

Northwest Press

An American publisher specializing in LGBT-themed comic books and graphic novels, founded in 2010 by Charles "Zan" Christensen. **northwestpress.com**

Queer Comics Expo

This annual event celebrates queer culture and promotes diverse queer representation in comics, animation and other great ways to tell stories. **qcexpo.tumblr.com**

Queers & Comics Conference

A biannual gathering of queer creators, scholars and fans. The location goes back and forth between NYC and San Francisco. **queersandcomics.cca.edu**

ADULT ENTERTAINMENT STORE

Feelmore Adult Gallery

If you live in or plan to visit Oakland, I highly recommend this adult entertainment store. Run by queer women of color, the selection of toys, books and art is well curated, and the customer service is exceptional. The owners are very knowledgeable and friendly to talk to and if they don't have exactly what you're looking for, they can order it for you. **1703 Telegraph Ave | feelmore510.com**

STORYTELLING SHOWS

Bawdy Storytelling

A live storytelling show and podcast that focuses on sex, kink, body image, and gender, run by sexual folklorist Dixie De la Tour. Smashes stigma and taboos and helps create an open, positive culture around sex. Plus it's a great place to meet people... **bawdystorytelling.com**

The Moth

Some of you know it as a podcast, but *The Moth* is also a live show in many cities. Put your name in the hat at the beginning of the show and you can tell a five-minute story on stage! Themes are preannounced ahead of time so you can work on and practice your story. It has to be true, about you, on theme, and within the time limit. I cannot recommend this highly enough. **themoth.org**

StorySlam Oakland

For folks in the Oakland area, I recommend this monthly open-mic and featured storytelling event, where people tell true personal stories on a theme. Prizes are awarded for the top two stories. Every Third Thursday at Sweet Bar Bakery, Oakland. **storyslamoakland.com**

WEB BLOG

lessonsfromtherps.com

The real-life Tina's excellent ongoing blog about lessons she learned in therapy. Check it out!

WRITING CLASSES

Writing Pad

I've learned a **ton** from this award-winning school. They offer classes and workshops in blogging, fiction, journalism, memoir, personal essay, storytelling and more in Los Angeles, San Francisco, and online. Their storytelling class set me up to succeed at *The Moth*, and their San Francisco home/writing workshop is beautiful. **writingpad.com**

FAVORITE PEN

For this book and others I have been using a Tombow Brush Pen.

BRUSH SIDE FOR DRAWING — PEN SIDE FOR WRITING

ACKNOWLEDGEMENTS

First and foremost, a huge thank you to my parents Cathy Beier and Thad Beier who have been incredibly supportive of me in every way. In my family it was always affirmed that it is okay to be queer, even before I came out at a relatively early age. My parents have also enthusiastically encouraged my art, including Mom copy editing all my work and Dad writing programs to help spot-clean my TIFF images. You're also very supportive and offer wise counsel and practical advice when I struggle, while always expressing confidence that I could lift myself up. Thank you for always being so excited and happy for me as I work towards my dreams.

I am also blessed with an incredibly loving and supportive family on both sides. Thank you Thomas, Pa and Nini, Grandpa and Kay, Aunt Ellen, Uncle Nik, Aunt Meg and Uncle Chris, Aunt Roberta, Uncle Jack, Aunt Ruth, Aunt Terry, Uncle George, Uncle John, Aunt Carol, and all my amazing cousins. I am glad we prioritize seeing each other as often as we do even though we live all across the country, and seeing you always makes me feel inspired and hopeful.

Thank you to Zan Christensen for sending that fateful email asking if I would like to create this anthology this summer and fund it through a Kickstarter Gold campaign. It's been an incredible opportunity to reach new audiences and push myself as an artist. I don't think I've ever had a period of time with such intense creative production and focus, and I'm thrilled to see it come together—having you and Northwest Press publish the book gave me a clear goal to strive for. I am learning and continue to learn a ton from you about how to promote a project, how to interact with fans, and the technical details of how to produce a great quality book. Thank you for facilitating this big leap forward in my art career.

Thank you to my editor K.J. Kelsch for giving me extensive help on this book, including critical feedback as I wrote my new material this summer (chapter 1 and 5-8), supporting me through the tougher emotional parts of writing the sad chapters, and doing a thorough content and copy edit of the full book. You knew exactly what I am trying to accomplish, but you also were able to see it from an aesthetic difference and critique it in a way I very much needed. As an editor you were able to spot both discrete mistakes in spelling or grammar and larger problems, thematically and structurally, and you also provided constructive solutions. Thanks for making the book the best it could be!

Thank you to Avery Trufelman from the *99% Invisible* podcast for writing such a beautiful foreword for the book. I love it, and you, to pieces.

Thank you to Demetria, Nina, Alfred, Joseph and all my other amazing friends—without your humor, wisdom, and playfulness, life would be no fun at all.

Thank you to Sara Ramirez for tweeting about the Kickstarter campaign while it was live, and for being a true champion for bisexuals both on and off screen.

Thank you to Alex Dueben for the full-length interview you did of me for *Smash Pages*. It was exciting and fun to present my project in my own words to the world, and you asked just the right questions to help facilitate that.

Thank you Jeff Bernstein and Marilyn Friedman for making such a beautiful creative class environment at the Writing Pad. Working with students serious about improving their craft, with instruction from brilliant teachers, greatly accelerated my learning and gave me a new community to grow with.

Thank you to the comics printer I used when I was still printing these comics myself—RA Comics Direct. For folks who don't have a publisher yet but would like a high-quality job with great customer service, I highly recommend them.

Thank you to my writing and storytelling teachers and mentors who have helped me find my voice: Corey Rosen, Dixie de la Tour, Davey Kim and Melissa Cistaro.

Thank you to my Sam Fox Art School Teachers and counselors, including Georgia Binnington, D.B. Dowd, John Hendrix, Jeff Pike, Dan Zettwoch, Jen Meyer, Mary Borgman, Tom Huck, and Sarah Birdsall. I think back to our assignments and what I learned from you regularly, especially the importance of graphic black shapes.

Thank you to my larger community of queer activists and artists who inspire me daily.

Thank you to my "therps" for keeping me sane and helping me take care of myself.

And finally, a **huge** thank you to my Kickstarter backers! (listed on next pages.)

None of this would have been possible without your timely monetary support. Thank you for pledging and sharing with your friends. I hope you love the book :)

Ace Edmonds, Adam O. Pruett, Adam Wagner, Adrian Roberts, Adriane Ruzak, Ajuna, Alenka F, Alex Martin, Alex Vitti, Alexa Patsalis, Alfred Schwab, Alicia lampkin, Amanda Stock, Amber, Amy Chu, Amy Jane Walker, Amy Lynn, Amy Thomas, André, Andrew Brouwer, Andrew Fones, Andrew Funk, Angela Brooks, Angela Gilbert, Angela Huang, Angela Pallatto Hockabout, Angelica Rosales, Annalisa, Annie McGrath, April Julier, Apurva Desai, Arielle, Armond Netherly, Avery, Awlbiste, Barbara, Bawdy Storytelling, ben poliak, Bernd Goetz, Betty Turbo, Bex, Bex Clark, Bob B., Bobb Waller, Bonnie Ricca, Branden Kornell, Brandon W. Stevens, Breanne, Brett Schmidt, Brian Calvary, Brian Madden, Brice Puls, Brittni Liyanage, Brookie Judge, Bruce Dunn, Bruce Shipman, C.G. Schroder, Caelyn McAulay, Caitlin McGuren, Caleb LaVergne, Callum Roper, Candace, Capellan, Cara Goldstein, Carmen Marin, Carol N, Cassandra Evans, Cat Hicks, Catharine Chen, Cathy Beier, Cayden, cdTHETHINGmarine, Cera Jackson, Charles Atencio, Charles Fitt, Charles Lobdell, Charlie Gage, Charlotte Nickel, Chelsea Robinson, Chiara Andriole, Chris Abele, Christa Barrett, Christine Turner, Christopher Law, Claire Ricketts, Claudia Berger, coleman, Comic Nurse, Contractor, CostaMuzzi, Craig Andersen, Curt Fortenbery, Curt Rissmiller, D.J. Trindle, Damien, Dana Kuhn, Dane Schnittman, Daniel Lin, Daniel Souweine, Daniela Lapidous, Dara Nigreville, David, David A Bopp, david deal, David Frahm, David Phan, David Raynaud, David Toccafondi, David Walter,

DB Dowd, Deborah Singer, Dee Morgan, Denis Lantsman, Dipanwita Pati, Dite Bray, Donna Prior, Duane McMullen, E. Pereira, Elaine Morgan, Eli Bishop, Elizabeth, Elizabeth Barcay, Elizabeth Sparks, Ellis Kim, elmonolav, Emerson, Emiliano Rios, Emily Jacobson, Emily January, Emily Lauren, Emma Barnes, Emma Brice, Eremon, Eric Starker, Erica McGillivray, Erica Schmitt, Erin Subramanian, ES, Esther J, Fabia White, Farah Ismail, Feasible Joint, Fer Goodnough, Flitterkit, Fossa, Frell, ftn, Gabrielle Shatan, Gearsoul Dragon, genester, Genevieve Allen, Georgia Binnington, Gina, Glaring Mistake, Grad Student, Greg McElhatton, (a number of "guest" logins), Halley Sanchez, Han Marshall, Hannah, Harald Niesche, hardtravelinghero, Heather, Heather Farrington, Heidi N, Henrik Hope, hep1013, Homenum Revelio, Hope Nicholson, Izzy Wow, J A, J F Traver, Jacob Lester, James Post, James Todd, Jan Frederiksen, Jason Gonding, Jason Marcy, Jason Olea, Jason Wagner, Jay Lofstead, Jeff Peterson, Jeffrey Pike, Jen, Jen Hiebert, Jenni Sands, Jennifer Ann Haubert, Jennifer Belknap, jennifer camper, Jennifer Knutson, Jennifer Ní HÉigeartaigh, Jenny Callahan Weinberg, Jeremy Owen, Jessica, Jessica Connor, Jessica Jones, Jessica Willson, Jetberry, Jillian Neustel, Jim Kosmicki, Joanie Macaroni, Joanne Ong, Jodie Ferries, Joe, Joe Dadek, john, John Boreczky, John Bx, John Hendrix, John Lustig, John Venzon, Jomicheal nelson, Josh Medin, Joshua Ballantyne, Julia, Julia Starkey, Julia Sutterfield McKinney, Julie Domitrek, Julie T Stalcup, Justin, Justin Hall, Karen Phung,

Kate Barton, Kate Goodin, Kathleen Reed, Katie, Katie, Katie Wills, Ken Gagne, Ken Hoffman, Kersh, Kevin J. Maroney, Kevin Matthews, Kevin McCarthy, Kevin Ward, Kimberley Long-Ewing, Kimberly Lynne, Kimberly M. Lowe, Kirsty Win, Kristi Taylor, Kristin Zumwalt, Kylar, Kym Dawson, Lara Taylor Kester, Laura Beckman, Laura Clements, Laurel Clausen, Lauren Chouinard, Lauren Featherston, Lauren Hoffman, Lauren Webb, Laurie Edwards, Leef Smith - "Mission: Comics & Art", Lenny, Leslie Sterling, lifetempo, Lillian, lillian white, Lily V, Liz Courts, LM, Lorrraine, M. York, Maddie Forrest, Manoël Trapier, Marcy Bain, Marian Swint, Marianne, Marie, Marie Kelly-Yuoh, Marinca, Marinda Huber, Marjorie Ornston, Mark Welch, Mark Wong, Martha Bass, Mary, Mary Anne Hinkle, Matilda Kirchen, Matt Miner, Matt Shand, Matthew Silady, Max Richie, Max Trense, Mccflute, McKinley Smoke, Meg, Megan Rose Gedris, Meghan Bortolon, Melinda Brown, Melissa Goldman, Menachem Cohen, Michael Georg Bregel, Michael Lachance, Michael Prior, Michael Scally, Michael Snook, Michelle Cerullo, Michelle Marsh, Michelle Schulz, MJ Wallace, Molly Haigh, Monika Pichler, MtFierce, Myles Fenlon, N. C. Christopher Couch, Nancy Marcus, Nanija, Natalie Patrice Tucker, Natasha Chisdes, Nathan Kellen, Naveen rajan, Neasa O'Sullivan, Nicholas George, Nicholas McBurney, Nick Nazar, NickS, Nikolas Swaner, Noel Schmidt, Nope Then, Nuria, Olivia, Olwen Lachowicz, Olympic Cards and Comics, Owlglass, Patrik Hanson, Pau Torrent, Paul Anderson, Paul Spence, Paula, Peg Duthie, Penny Gronbeck, Peter Strömberg, PF Anderson, PhoenixTerran, Pilar Mejia, Purple Parfait, Rachael Elizabeth Evans Summers, Rachel, Rachel Chaney, Rachel Krislov, Rachel Mc Veigh, Rachel V McKinnon, Randall Nichols, Randy Flynn, Raymond McCauley, Rebecca Horner, Red L, Regina Lipp, Remo Stirnimann, Ren Barker, Rhianna Zuby, Rhiannon, Rob McMonigal, Rob Vincent, Robert Lucien Howe, Roberta Gregory, Robin Dolan, Robyn Adams, Rory Polanco, Ruth Beier, Sally Rose, Samantha Beiko, Samantha Netzley, Sami, Sara Moore, Sarah, Sarah Birdsall, Sarah Liberman, Sarah Mahoney, Sarah Morrison, Sarah Searls, Sarah Stewart, Sarah Stumpf, School of Visual Arts Library, scott mitchell rosenberg, Scott Shillcock, SecretBaroness, Seren Ser, serena dv, ShadowCub, Shail Maingi, Shana Sessler, Sharon, Sharon Nolan, Shelley Dodge, simon, Single Helix Studios, Sonya Saturday, Sophie Forsyth, Sophie Mendelson, starmaru, Still Fighting, Sue-Rae Rosenfeld, SwitchDoc Labs, Tam, Tamaria Rose Lavelle, Tania, Tara Avery, Tara Morrigan, Tasha Turner Lennhoff, Taylor Scoma, Ted Abenheim, Theresa, Thomas BOURKE, Thomas Werner, Tiffany Marcheterre, Tim Murray, Tina Klassen, Tobias Fleischer // PYLON.FM Productions, Tom B., Torborg, Trystan Vel, Tsz-Lung, Turbanous, Tyger, tyler cohen, Tyson Vanover, V. Garlock, Valerie Storey, vampyric kitty, Vera Weiß, Veronica Michaelsen, Vic, Vicky McNair, Vida Cruz, Walter Gordon, William nelson, William O. Tyler, willie, Yawmin Jie, ykarie

ABOUT *the* AUTHOR

Elizabeth Beier is an artist, cartoonist, and storyteller based in San José, California. She has been working on these *Bisexual Trials and Errors* comics since 2014, although she produced over a third of it in Summer 2017.

Elizabeth's next big project will be a graphic memoir about middle school and having a crush on her best friend. She is also exploring creating shorter journalistic comics. One of her strengths as an artist is "live" drawing, speedily capturing words, portraits, and actions as they take place.

Her favorite kind of drawing pen, as of September 2017, is an N15 Tombow Brush Pen.

Stories about her work have appeared in *SF Gate*, *MTV News*, *Smash Pages*, *Book Riot*, *Comics Alliance*, and *The Comics Journal*.

Elizabeth performs at story-telling shows including *The Moth*, *Bawdy Storytelling*, *Oakland Story Slam*, and more. In March of 2016, she won a Berkeley Moth Story Slam with the theme "Witness", and performed at the Castro Theater for the Grand Slam in October 2016.

Elizabeth believes art can be a force for positive change. After winning the Prism Comics Queer Press Grant in 2016, she joined the nonprofit's board as the Grant chair. More info can be found on Prism Comics in the Resources section of this book.

To learn more about Elizabeth and her art, please visit **elizabethdrewyou.com**. You can contact her at **beier.elizabeth@gmail.com**. Feel free to reach out.